CRAFTING
WITH
Nature

GROW OR GATHER YOUR OWN SUPPLIES FOR SIMPLE HANDMADE CRAFTS, GIFTS & RECIPES

AMY RENEA

FOUNDER OF A NEST FOR ALL SEASONS—
THE READER'S CHOICE WINNER OF *BETTER HOMES AND GARDENS*
BLOGGER AWARDS IN GARDENING

PAGE STREET
PUBLISHING CO.

DEDICATION

To my four little ones, who say crafting from nature is one of their favorite things.

PAGE STREET
PUBLISHING CO.

First published in 2016 by
Page Street Publishing Co.
27 Congress Street, Suite 103
Salem, MA 01970
www.pagestreetpublishing.com

Distributed by Macmillan, sales in Canada by The Canadian Manda Group.

19   18   17   16   1   2   3   4   5

ISBN-13: 978-1-62414-198-0
ISBN-10: 1-62414-198-6

Library of Congress Control Number: 2015953960

Cover and book design by Page Street Publishing Co.
Photography by Amy Renea

Printed and bound in China

Page Street is proud to be a member of 1% for the Planet. Members donate one percent of their sales to one or more of the over 1,500 environmental and sustainability charities across the globe who participate in this program.

WHAT PEOPLE ARE SAYING ABOUT
CRAFTING WITH NATURE

"This book belongs in the collection of every self-respecting gardener or crafter who takes great pride in creating something special with their own hands!"

—BARBARA CORCORAN, owner of the crafty clothing company Grace & Lace and star of ABC's *Shark Tank*

"*Crafting with Nature* brings me back to my childhood and all of the natural products and remedies I used to make. The crafts look beautiful yet easy to do, and the photography is gorgeous! I cannot wait to dig in with my children! Truly inspiring."

—LAUREN LIESS, founder of Pure Style Home and author of *Habitat: The Field Guide to Decorating*

"Pinterest comes to your backyard in this naturo-inspired workbook full of beautiful handmade items. This book is a must-read for the creative folks who don't mind getting their hands dirty."

—BETH BRYAN, founder of Unskinny Boppy

"This book has become THE reference guide for how to maximize my efforts in being a better gardener and crafter. Amy has demystified the processes involved in sourcing supplies and provided simple, step-by-step directions to create usable art. This is garden and craft alchemy at its best!"

—JENNIFER CARROL, founder of *Celebrating Everyday Life* magazine

"This book takes 'reduce, reuse and recycle' to the next level of beautiful. Making fun from nature is a great way to live a little greener—a must-have book for year-round crafting."

—SHAWNA CORONADO, author of *Grow a Living Wall*

"As someone who grows lots of herbs and flowers, loves crafts and making natural products for my home, this book speaks volumes to me. What better way to be crafty than by collecting or growing the materials yourself? Amy has written a winner!"

—LISA STEELE, author of *Fresh Eggs Daily*

"Reading the tutorials in this book can help inspire and enable gardeners and crafters alike to use their plants in new and creative ways."

—BALL HORTICULTURAL COMPANY

"So many people fail to use the plants in their garden. Plants are so much more than just a bunch of pretty petals. Amy's crafty garden tutorials will help you discover a whole new layer of appreciation and pride in your garden."

—ROCHELLE GREAYER, founder of Pith + Vigor and author of *Cultivating Garden Style*

"*Crafting with Nature* is an invaluable source of inspiration and information for anyone passionate about creativity."

—MELISSA RIKER, founder of The Happier Homemaker

contents

section six
GROW A HAND-CRAFTED CHRISTMAS CELEBRATION   171

HOW TO USE THIS BOOK

You might crack open this book and wonder whether it is written for crafters or gardeners. I will hastily answer back *both*! I have written these grow guides and these tutorials for the makers. For the creatives who want to craft with their hands and the growers who want to get their hands dirty, this book is for you. I want the garden lovers to get bitten by the crafting bug and I want the crafty folk to start growing their own craft supplies. I want the makers to make. I want you to grow and make and make and grow and do it all again. There is nothing so rewarding as creating something with your very own hands, and to create with what you have grown is doubly so.

In each chapter, there will be a grow or gather guide, chart or explanation about certain plants or natural crafting materials. I have chosen plants that are fairly easy to grow and materials that are fairly easy to find so that everyone can be successful. No one enjoys failing on the first attempt, so these plants will give you confidence and help you move on to more difficult and fussy natural crafting materials. Note that some chapters branch out into natural materials you find both outdoors in the woods and indoors in your pantry. These natural materials are free or cheap for the taking and can often be combined with plant materials for fun and functional crafts.

The latter part of each chapter will give you ideas for creating both practical and pretty DIYs with your grown and gathered supplies. Some projects require a full photo-tutorial while others are simply an idea to inspire you. My hope is that you do not simply follow my instructions and call it a day. My sincere hope is that you take these fresh ideas, thought-out methods and these base crafting recipes, and then mix them up with your own creativity. Change up lemongrass for a mixture of tangerine and orange or substitute a richer deeper beeswax for the bleached version I used. Make 100 tiny little wreaths instead of one large one like mine. Experiment. Enjoy. Entertain the idea that I am simply opening a door for crafting with materials that you grow or gather yourself.

Once you have opened the door to creating with natural materials, consider gifting the fruits of your labor. Most of these projects make wonderfully sweet little hostess gifts, birthday tokens or simply a little package to say, "I am thinking of you." Most of the projects are consumable, crying out to be *used* and will not clutter up your friend's home with gifts she cannot use. Many of the gifts can simply be tossed onto the compost pile when they have lost their usefulness or luster. From the earth they come and back to dust they return. It is a wonderful way to craft and I hope you join me as we dive in feet first.

To find more details, photos, projects and shopping lists, visit CraftingWithNature.com.

section one

BEGINNER PLANTS TO GATHER, GROW & CRAFT

Have you opened this book worried that you might have bitten off more than you can chew? Perhaps you love crafting, but plants always seem to die on you. Perhaps you are the garden girl who manages to grow amazing produce to give to your friends, but you wouldn't call your gift giving particularly "pretty." Maybe you are scared of both gardening and crafting, but you are drawn to both of them creatively. If any of those scenarios describes you, then this section of garden crafts is specifically for you. These three chapters are meant to be relatively easy, with a high rate of staggering success! I want you to dip your toes into this wonderful world of growing your own craft materials and I want you to be prepared to dive in by the end.

I hope these three chapters get you excited about growing, crafting and giving away your creations! You will learn how to care for and gift little mini-moss gardens, jars full of jewel-toned jellies and jams and some rosemary soap bars or scented salts. These plants are accessible, the crafting supplies are readily available and inexpensive and the methods are straightforward. Are you ready to begin? We start with moss and fairies...

CHAPTER 1

MOSS HISTORIES & FAIRY MYSTERIES

When you want to begin crafting with natural materials, you should pick plants that are readily available, easy to grow and easy to maintain. Moss is a perfect candidate. In this chapter, I will give you an introduction to the plant itself, and then dive straight into the world of fairy gardens, moss rocks and miniature décor. Let's start with the plant though, shall we?

HOW TO GATHER AND TRANSPLANT MOSS

Moss is as old as sin. Hanging with its woodland bedfellow, the fern, moss has quite possibly been around since the dawn of time. It is different from most plants in several ways.

» It grows very, very slowly.

» Moss does not have roots that penetrate the soil. Rather, it connects to a substrate via short rhizoids. Think of these like little pieces of Velcro holding the moss onto a rock or tree trunk, rather than feeding tubes for the plant.

» Moss gets most of its nutrients through its leaves and from the water it absorbs, not from roots in rich soil

» Moss has no flowers. (Sad, I know!)

» Moss reproduces via spores—not seeds. You will sometimes see moss with what looks like tiny stems and flowers, but those are called "capsules" and they contain the spores. Moss relies on wind to burst open the capsules and transport the spores to create new colonies.

What does all of that mean for you, the beginner gardeners, the fairy aficionados and the natural crafting crowd? Well, it means you have to give moss what it wants, and what it wants is often much different than a typical plant. When you want to collect moss for a project, there are two very important things to remember

DO NOT DIG! SLICE OR SCRUNCH INSTEAD

There are two basic methods to collecting moss: slice or scrunch. When moss is very wet, slicing works best, but when dry, it can simply be scrunched off its rock or bark. To slice, simply take a trowel or hori hori and horizontally detach the rhizoids near the soil, bark or rock. Attempt to keep the moss clump as intact as possible. Immediately transport the moss to a similar planting environment and water it in.

To scrunch the moss, use a gentle pressure with your fingers on the top of the moss, as if you were shampooing your hair. Many mosses will detach very easily and scrunching helps to keep the clumps intact. Again, move to a new environment quickly and water well.

TAKE A LITTLE, LEAVE A LOT

Though moss is often considered a weed and certainly not lacking in *my* woods, I still have a responsibility to leave the woodland environment with as little damage and loss as possible. Therefore, I collect from "weedy" locations first, like the lawn. I also try to go by a 10 percent rule for each variety of plant while collecting. If there are 100 clumps of cushion moss along the stream, I will take 10 or so. If there are only 10 clumps of fern moss, well, I only get 1. If you are collecting moss from an area that is about to be demolished or developed, feel free to collect all that is available.

TYPES OF MOSS

There are thousands of species of moss, but we will focus on a few common types crafters and gardeners love—especially those that are good for fairy gardens.

1. **Rock-cap moss.** These are tough mosses that grow directly on rocks. (See more about moss rocks on the next page.) Use them directly on rocks as accents in the fairy garden or use large moss rocks to anchor a scene.

2. **Fern moss.** This moss predictably looks like a carpet of ferns that spreads laterally over the surface of the soil. Fern moss makes a fabulous forest floor base for fairies, mimicking human scaled ferns on a woodland path.

3. **Cushion moss.** These adorable little clumps that look like fairy cushions are my favorite! Use these little puffs of moss in mini-gardens, as accents against flatter mosses and in groups to look like rolling hillsides of grass.

4. **Spoon moss.** Use this moss in "sheets" to cover soil, drape over fairy rooftops or to create a tiny "lawn."

5. **Tree moss.** This moss has little "trees" that grow out of a flatter base layer, making it perfect for creating a bit of height in a fairy garden. This type also absorbs quite a bit more than other types of moss, making it perfect for small containers that you are worried about overflowing.

6. **Log moss.** Contrary to tree moss, log moss does not look like trees. Rather, it *grows* on trees—particularly dead, rotting logs. It grows quickly (for moss), so if you find some, you can take more than what my 10 percent rule usually allows. It can be weedier than most moss, so craft away heartily!

MYTHS ABOUT MOSS

Moss always needs deep shade. FALSE. Though mosses love growing on the woodland floor, they do need sun! Some varieties actually need quite a bit of light to thrive. A rule of thumb is to simply give your moss a similar environment from whence it came.

All moss needs to be wet all the time. FALSE. Although many mosses thrive in moist environments and they all need water to survive, they do not need water all the time. In fact, acrocarps—one of the two major types of moss—must dry out periodically to thrive.

Moss only grows on the North side of trees. FALSE. While moss often grows on the northern side of trees, it will also grow on the East, West and South. Moss loves shade and will grow anywhere it can find it. The Northern side of a house or tree is often the shadiest spot, but it is not necessarily the only shaded location available.

HOW TO COLLECT AND MAINTAIN MOSS ROCKS

My favorite way to collect moss is to collect its full habitat. Mosses often grow on beautiful rocks or on bark, typically on the forest floor. Collecting rocks and bark with moss already growing is an easier way to get instant atmosphere in your fairy gardens as well as maintaining the environment where the moss is "happy." Most "moss failures" occur when moss is collected and then placed in an environment where it cannot thrive. Lack of water, lack of light and the change of host environment can really deal a deathly blow to moss. Whether you collect moss rocks for fairy gardens or simply as accents to your garden pots and paths, they are a charming addition.

Gloves (optional)

Large bucket

Water source or gallon jug of water

NOTE: Some moss rocks have tiny little colonies just beginning while others have thick, thriving moss. Try a combination of the different types for a varied garden landscape or stick with one type for a striking planter! Also, remember to take small amounts of the current moss colony when collecting, leaving plenty of each variety in the woods to continue propagating naturally.

1. When you decide to hunt down moss rocks, it's a good idea to bring gloves along so that the rocks don't fall out of your hands and onto your feet! The rocks are very slippery! This is especially true if little ones are assisting to gather the moss rocks. You also want a large bucket for hauling your rocks with water to keep the moss moist. If you are not going to be gathering the moss rocks from a place near a natural water source like a stream or lake, bring along a gallon jug of water.

2. Look for moss rocks in a shallow creek bed, under little "coves" on creek banks and throughout cool woodland terrain. Look for very large colonies of moss on and nearby the rock, and only take a small portion (up to 10 percent) of that colony.

3. Once you find your moss rocks, lift up gently from the bottom without touching the moss on top. Place gently into your bucket and keep moist with a small amount of water. The rocks do not need to be submerged, but should stay moist to the touch.

4. After collecting moss rocks, give them a home that mimics their environment in a cool, shaded place. Moisture is a must, so a pot that is watered daily, a fountain that sprays its surroundings or even a man-made stream are all good options! Remember that if you are using an acrocarp, the moss must dry out once a week or so and cannot constantly be wet.

5. To maintain your rocks, check every other day or so that there is moisture getting to the moss. There is no need to feed the moss. If the moss starts to turn brown, that is a sign that it is getting too much sun and/or not enough moisture. Change the location or add additional moisture to green it up again!

MINIATURE FAIRY GARDENS

Moss suits itself perfectly as the base for fairy gardens. Fairy gardens are themed gardens that operate under the assumption that imaginary fairies have taken up residence. They can be made in a portion of a traditional outdoor garden or set up as tiny miniature gardens in a pot. The basic components are typically moss, twigs, branches and bark structures, moss rocks and tiny accessories.

Fairy gardens need not be complicated, time consuming or expensive. While you can spend hundreds of dollars collecting fairy garden "supplies," I think the most rewarding fairy gardens are often the tiny ones. Little hidden fairy hideouts are unexpected, inexpensive and easy enough for children to assemble.

Container

Enough potting soil to mostly fill container

Collected moss specimens and moss rocks (see page 14)

Collected bits and baubles

1. Start with a simple container. It can be anything—natural cavities in a chunk of wood, a thrift store ceramic find or a recycling bin rescue. It can even be broken or chipped, though beware the tiny hands of children around sharp edges. The only requirement fairies dictate is that it must be cute.

2. Fill ¾ of your container with potting soil and then add in complementary moss and/or moss rocks. I think of your moss and containers first and foremost as shapes. Are you connecting two pieces of a circle with a rounded bowl and cushion moss? Are you creating an arching bridge of moss over a bent bark log? How will the moss continue or complement the lines of your container?

3. Once you have arranged your moss so that it is pleasing to the eye, give the planter a good shower of water. I typically give new planters a few waterings in the sink or outdoors with a watering can, so that they can get a good dunking with water saturating the moss and the soil, eventually running out the bottom of the planter. If your container does not have a drainage hole, you can use a power drill or hammer and nails to create several small holes in the bottom for drainage. If that's not possible, you still want to give it a good soaking, but make sure there is no water sitting in the bottom of the container. Allow it to dry out before watering again.

4. The third and final component of these miniature gardens is perhaps the most fun— decorating! Collect various little bits and baubles from the woods, the junk drawer or the toy box to adorn the garden and attract fairies.

(continued)

MINIATURE FAIRY GARDENS (CONTINUED)

Acorn tops, twigs, bits of rope, shiny marbles or little charms are all a good place to start. Consider creating furniture sets out of twigs, housing out of chunks of bark and fairy home accessories from the dregs of your child's toy collection. Keep in mind that fairies love all things tiny and adorable! Refer to the provided photos for super easy and fun decorations.

Consider your fairy to be a bit like Mr. Elf on the Shelf. Fairies can be whimsical and ridiculous, cute and flirty or plain old petulant. It is fun to create environments for different fairy personalities. Why not create a fairy farm? Perhaps a tiny fairy tends a "farm" of dinosaur eggs! Weird? Yes. Fun? *Yes!* Consider the glamorous and Oz-loving fairies that might create an Emerald City. Complete with green glass bottles, painted glass and moss accents, a miniature Emerald City speaks to a more ambitious and beauty-seeking fairy, don't you think? Of course, there are the utilitarian fairies who prefer good old cement. Perhaps these fairies set up housekeeping in small cement planters all stacked in a row!

The opportunities and ideas are endless and this open-ended creative environment is perfect to allow children to exercise their imaginations! Whichever kind of fairy inhabits your garden, make sure the moss stays moist.

Once I have created these tiny hideouts, I like to place them where they are completely unexpected. A bright blue teapot with moss spilling off all sides finds a home just off the garden path while a ten-cent bowl filled high with cushion moss makes the perfect seat for a fairy finding room under a bench. Rather than broadcasting their location to the world, fairies like their privacy!

These mini-gardens are beautiful in the home, too. Of course, place them in partially hidden parts of a room to be mindful of the fairies' privacy. Your children will love the idea of inviting fairies into your home and trying to catch a glimpse of glitter or the whisper of their wings as they fly out of sight!

NOTE: You need not be limited in creativity or by cost when building fairy gardens! Here are a few ideas to kick-start your creativity using natural (free!) materials for fairy garden accessories.

Acorn Cap + Twig = Fairy Mushrooms or Trees

Double Acorn Cap + Marble = Fairy Sconce

Acorn Caps + Acorn Caps = Rain Chains or Rooftops

Maple Seed "Helicopters" = Fairy Wings

Two Large Branches + Tiny Sticks = Fairy Ladder

Jenga Pieces + String = Fairy Bridge

Wood Slices + Wood Pieces = Fairy Tables

THE FAIRY GARDEN HUB

If you have access to a woodland environment or creek, you can really go all out with a fairy "hub," so to speak. All those little fairy hideouts are for individual fairies or small families of fairies, but when the fairies get together, they can create quite a city! Moss rocks, large ladders (for those who have broken their wings), cobbled pathways of acorn caps—these are all signs that you have stumbled upon a fairy hub!

Suitable site (see note below)

Various types of moss

Hand trowel and garden fork

Old kitchen spoon, knife and fork (optional)

Various sizes of twigs

Acorn caps, seed pods and other woodland detritus

Old toys, game pieces and/or fairy garden furniture and accessories

NOTE: Fairy gardens can be created anywhere you please, but I think they look best in a woodland garden near a water source. Whether that is a creek, a small pool, a waterfall or a tiny trickle from a crack in a boulder, the sight and sound of water makes things a bit more magical. A water source will also make sure the moss in your garden does not dry out and die. It also makes your garden a bit more prone to flooding, so make sure you locate your garden on slightly higher ground near the water source. For my fairy garden hub, I chose a little island poking out of a small creek. You also want to consider foot traffic from both humans and animals. You want visitors to be able to see your garden without accidentally stepping on it!

1. After choosing a suitable location, assess the topographical qualities that are already available in the space. Is there a notch in a tree that looks like a fairy door? Is there a mound of virgin soil where moss could easily drape across and form hillocks? Are there rocks covered in moss that could be repositioned to make a garden wall? Use your imagination to see with "builders'" eyes.

2. Once you have taken stock of the area, decide what your basic layout will be. Will you have a central fairy house with various outbuildings, or will you make a small city with many small fairy huts? Will your garden extend up into a tree or stay on the ground? How will you use the water source? Use a twig to make a general outline in the soil of your rough city plan.

3. Once your outline is complete, you must consider the water source a bit more carefully. Are there already clues to how the water expands when it rains? Check for bare spots or collections of rocks with just one or two small plants. Check for trees with exposed roots on the creek banks. These are signs that those particular areas will flood when it rains. Alternatively, big patches of grass indicate that flooding does not happen very often.

4. Start building your garden literally from the ground up. Transplant the mosses you have collected onto bare patches of soil or create bare patches by using the trowel to clear the soil and a garden fork to gently rake it. If you do not have garden tools, a kitchen knife can cut moss to transplant, a kitchen spoon can scoop soil and a kitchen fork can rake the soil. Water in all moss thoroughly.

5. Once the basic "land" is laid out, it is time to consider fences and large structures. Fencing gives a more defined look to your fairy garden and can be created from a variety of materials. Little twigs or wood skewers make great posts and basic cotton string or hemp can be added to create crossbeams. Lash twigs together with string to make ladders and bridges, which make strong vertical and horizontal lines within the garden. If you'd like to make large "bark houses" or other significant structures, now is the time to site them.

6. Once the basic structures and topographical features are set, then you get to have fun decorating! Add in carved wooden fairy doors, little acorn-topped totems, various miniature garden accessories and signs hand-painted by the "fairies"! See page 20 for photos and ideas for these smaller fairy garden accessories.

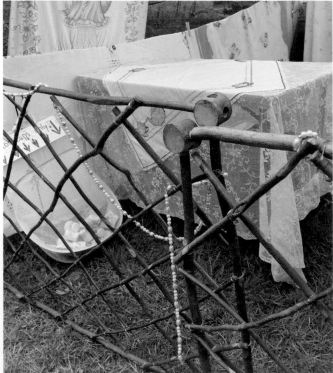

CHAPTER 2

ROSEMARY FOR REMEMBRANCE

Have you ever rubbed your hands up against a sprig of fresh rosemary? If not, it is one of the simplest pleasures in life and I beseech you to get yourself to a rosemary bush and *inhale*. The scent of rosemary is not one for those tender of the nose, nor is it for those who like a quick and fleeting olfactory experience. No, rosemary is an herb that sticks with you quite literally. Perhaps that is why Shakespeare so famously characterized this common herb as the herb for remembrance. This scent makes rosemary the perfect herb to include for both toilette and culinary applications. Join me as I show you how to make simple scented salt and infused oil and the more complex rinses and soaps of rosemary.

HOW TO GROW AND CARE FOR ROSEMARY

Rosemary is a Mediterranean plant, meaning it likes a nice temperate climate, plenty of light and no soggy feet! Rosemary is very difficult to grow from seed, so start with a small plant from your local nursery. Repot in a slightly larger pot with rich potting soil mixed with one cup of sand for drainage.

Rosemary can be a bit finicky as a houseplant because it is easy to err on the over watering *or* under watering side of things. The best advice I can give you is to *soak* and *dry* every two weeks or so. Instead of watering every day or forgetting to water for weeks on end, a good soak and dry will keep your rosemary happy. Simply place the pot in a large sink and give the entire plant a good soaking until water runs out the bottom of the pot. Once the pot stops dripping (after several hours), take the plant back to a sunny location and leave it alone for a week. Allow the roots to just start drying out, and water again when the top 2 to 3 inches (5 to 7.5 cm) of soil starts to get dry.

Rosemary also benefits from a good pruning now and then. When pruning, take no more than a third of the plant to encourage new growth, give a more rounded appearance or to utilize the herb in cooking or crafts. When I prune rosemary, I take small stems, strip most of the leaves for cooking or crafts, then sink those naked stems into a pot. You would be surprised how many times those simple little "throw-away" stems turn into new little rosemary plants! Perfect for potting up in a new little pot as a gift for a friend!

HOW TO MAKE ROSEMARY-SCENTED SALT AND INFUSED OLIVE OIL

When we were first married, I tried very hard to be the perfect wife. I made many "fancy" dishes in the kitchen that came out smelling amazing, but my husband would only eat a few tiny bites. Though I am certainly not a gourmet chef, I couldn't understand why he wouldn't eat more of the delicious Focaccia bread or roasted potatoes I was slaving away over! The answer? With the kindness of a bewildered new husband, he asked, "Why are there pine needles in them?" Well, those pine needles were rosemary. While I agreed the texture of rosemary needles is not the most pleasant, the smells were so intoxicating and the finished products were so beautiful that I couldn't believe he didn't want to eat them! Needless to say, I took rosemary off the menu for a while, until I realized a simple truth. You can have your rosemary and eat it too! The flavor of rosemary can be infused into salts and oils, allowing cooks to utilize that delicious taste without the "pine needle" effect.

Typically making herbal or vegetable powders requires a dehumidifier. Rosemary, however, is special. That remarkable smell is so memorable because is it incredibly concentrated. There is not a huge amount of moisture in rosemary leaves to begin with, so drying them out in preparation for powder is not that difficult. Making the scented salt is simple—just flip to the next page to learn how! See page 25 to learn how to infuse rosemary into olive oil.

Various oils such as olive, walnut or sunflower oil can be used to create flavored artisan oils.

SEVEN QUICK STEPS
FOR ROSEMARY-SCENTED SALT

1. Cut five or six foot-long (30.5 cm) branches of rosemary (or the equivalent amount of small pieces)

2. Hang in bunches, or lay in a large bowl to dry for one week or until leaves begin to shed.

3. Strip leaves by moving your fingers downwards along the stem, against the growth of the leaves, and add to blender. Leaves should fill blender about halfway.

4. Combine leaves with ½ cup (135 g) of salt in the blender. Pulse blender for 5 minutes or until rosemary is broken into small pieces and fully integrated with salt.

5. Decant through a strainer into a clean jar or bowl.

6. Push the mixture against the strainer to capture as much salt and rosemary oil as possible. Seal your jar and allow it to cure for 1 week.

7. Decant salt and any rosemary powder into a pretty jar through a sieve. Discard the remaining large pieces.

NOTE: In recipes, you may substitute salt for this homemade rosemary salt.

ROSEMARY-INFUSED OLIVE OIL

Creating infused olive oils is slightly more intensive than salts, simply because the salt cuts down on any potential bacteria while the oils do not. Thus, you must be more careful about sterilization and dryness when making infused oils. The first thing you must do is clean your herbs and spices and allow to fully dry. When it comes to plants like rosemary, lavender or rose hips, this means allowing them to hang and dry completely for a week or two. For spices and seeds that have already been dried out on the stalk, simply pluck them from the plant, store them in a clean, dry container and they are good to go!

Sterilize your jars in a boiling water bath, being careful to pick them up with proper canning tongs. Again, make sure they dry completely. Fill the jar loosely with large herb stems or use 2 to 3 tablespoons (20 to 30 g) of seeds such as fennel or coriander. Pour extra-virgin olive oil over the herbs and spices to the top of the jar. Close the jar, and allow the volatile herb oils to infuse the olive oil for 1 to 2 weeks. You can taste the oil as it infuses to see how strong it has become. Strain the herbs from the oil once the flavor is strong as they can grow moldy and botulism can be an issue. Use the oil immediately for cooking, store in the refrigerator or utilize for creating bath and beauty products! If you are gifting infused oils, play it safe by including a "use by" date within a few months of creating the oil.

Many other herbs, spices and peppers can be infused in oils this way. Here are a few of my favorite combinations for gifting at Christmas time and throughout the year as hostess gifts.

- » Chili pepper and allspice
- » Clove, allspice and a cinnamon stick
- » Star anise and licorice root
- » Rosemary and thyme
- » Lavender and rosehip

- » Coriander, cumin and fennel
- » Mustard, dill and caraway
- » Paprika and turmeric
- » Lemongrass and lime zest
- » Garlic, serrano pepper and poblano seed

Both the infused oil and DIY salt make fantastic little gifts, particularly for a host or hostess around the holidays. Perhaps you could gift the foodie in your life a beautiful bottle of infused oil complete with a loaf of fresh baked bread or package rosemary salts in a pretty wooden salt cellar. You could even include both along with a pretty potted rosemary plant for a beloved family member or friend.

INFUSED OIL TROUBLESHOOTING

My oil is cloudy! What happened? Olive oil can become cloudy naturally, particularly when cool. If the oil is in the refrigerator, set it out and see if the cloudiness clears up. If the cloudiness does not clear up, then the oil has turned rancid and must be tossed out.

The rosemary in my oil is turning black and soft. What should I do? You should have removed the rosemary once the oils have infused. If the herb is black, it has become moldy and you must throw that batch out due to the risk of botulism that occurs with all canning ventures.

The flavor of my oil seems "off." What did I do wrong? Well, it depends on how old your oil is and how it has been stored. If you will use oil over a long time period, consider storing it in the refrigerator. Also, if oil is to be kept for a long time, you will want to use a dark colored bottle to prevent the degradation of the oil. If you have stored the oil properly and it still tastes off, the herbs might not have been dry enough and might have molded.

DIY ROSEMARY HAIR RINSES

Rosemary salts are safe and rosemary oils are a bit more tricky. Rosemary rinses fall somewhere right in the middle. Made from either water or vinegar and herbal oils, rinses are a great home DIY craft project for the beginner. The rinses are a great natural way to darken hair, add shine and give your hair a wonderful, natural scent!

YIELD—1 (16-OZ [473-ML]) JAR

4 to 5 fresh sprigs of rosemary

16-oz (473-ml) canning jar

Boiling water

1. Start with the fresh rosemary in a clean canning jar and put some water onto the stove to boil. It is important to use canning jars, as hot water can cause lightweight glass containers to shatter.

2. Once your water comes to a boil, allow it to cool for 5 minutes and then pour directly into the canning jar over the sprigs of rosemary, about 1 inch (2.5 cm) from the rim of the jar.

3. Allow the jar to cool for 30 to 60 minutes, then seal the jar. The water will turn dark from the rosemary, and that is one of the benefits! Rosemary rinses have been known to both darken hair and also benefit hair growth. While there are no scientific studies supporting these benefits, there is one thing that is certain—your hair will smell amazing!

WEB SOURCES

Apple-Cider-Vinegar-Benefits.com (apple-cider-vinegar-benefits.com/natural-hair-care-product.html)

ROSEMARY HAIR RINSE VARIATIONS

Apple cider vinegar. Apple cider vinegar has been known to close the hair shaft, making your hair super shiny! Mix 1 part vinegar with 3 parts hot water over your rosemary leaves. Don't worry, the vinegar smell disappears when hair dries, but the rosemary scent lingers.

White vinegar and chamomile. If you are a blonde, you might want to try this rinse! The white vinegar acts as a boost for shiny hair, while the chamomile is known to lighten color. Rosemary will counteract this effect with its slight darkening properties, so beware that hair might slightly darken overall. Use 1 part vinegar to 3 parts chamomile tea poured over rosemary leaves.

Beet juice. This rinse is for the redheads! Rosemary alone will darken hair color, but the addition of a little beet juice slightly refreshes red hair color.

ROSEMARY RINSE FOR REDS

ROSEMARY HAIR RINSE FOR BLONDES

ROSEMARY SOAP BARS

Rosemary makes a great addition to soap bars, particularly for exfoliating or scrubbing soaps. I love gifting these types of soaps to my gardening friends, because goodness knows we need a bit of scrubbing on our hands after working in the dirt for a few hours! This gardener's soap includes crushed allspice and rosemary leaves with an extra hit of fragrant rosemary oil. It is a beautiful clear soap with gritty bits of herb and spice, perfect for rough, dry and dirty hands.

YIELD—12 SOAP BARS

Knife

1 lb (454 g) slab glycerin soap base

Microwave-safe bowl

½ cup (40–60 g) dry rosemary leaves

¼ cup (20–30 g) whole allspice berries

10 to 30 drops rosemary essential oil

Silicone loaf pan

1. With a dull kitchen knife, cut your soap base into small chunks, about 2 square inches (5 cm) in size.

2. Place the chunks into a microwave-safe bowl and heat 30 seconds at a time until the soap is fully melted. Give the mix a little stir with a wooden spoon every two heatings or so to make sure it is evenly heating. Do not allow the soap to boil. Alternatively, you can allow the soap to melt in a double boiler or small crafting crockpot.

3. While the soap is melting, strip the rosemary leaves from the stem. Place the leaves and allspice into a plastic bag and crush with a meat tenderizer. Alternatively, you can reduce the rosemary to powder in a food processer.

4. Mix the rosemary powder and allspice bits in with the melted soap and add up to 30 drops of rosemary essential oil or any complementary essential oil of your choice.

5. Carefully pour the soap mixture into a silicone loaf pan or molding container of your choice. Work slowly and gently as the hot soap can burn viciously.

6. Allow the soap to completely cool and harden. This can take up to 24 hours depending on the size of your mold. You will notice that the rosemary powder offers a beautiful green tint to the glycerin while the larger chunks of allspice sink to the bottom of the soap.

7. Once cool and hardened, pop the soap out of the mold and cut into bars with a sharp knife.

NOTE: One slab of soap base works with ½ cup (40 to 60 g) fresh rosemary and up to 30 drops of essential oil for a full loaf pan. If you are making a smaller batch and/or using smaller molds, use less rosemary accordingly.

EDIBLE CLIMBING VINES & CANES TO SNACK & CRAFT

When you walk into a garden, sometimes things just "feel right" and other times, something feels a bit off. A garden needs both height and movement, and there are very few plants that can provide both. Large mature trees provide height, but take many years to grow. When you want to fill a vertical space quickly, you want a vine or caning plant. Almost any vine will work, but edibles are my favorite. Blackberries and grapevines are high at the top of the list. You might also consider a flowering vine such as clematis (pictured), climbing hydrangea or the classic climbing rose, but here we focus on the edibles.

These edibles not only provide vertical interest, but provide jewel-like fruits that make delicious homemade condiments or snacks straight off the vine! Not only can you eat the fruits of your labor, but the vines themselves make fantastic crafting material. In this chapter we will dive into the world of grapevine crafts with pretty and functional ornaments for your garden.

HOW TO GROW AND GUIDE EDIBLE CLIMBING VINES

Many vines are quite tough, even when they look rather fragile. They have a few requirements that will help them thrive. First and foremost, you must note the *type* of vine you are growing and how it attaches itself to climb.

TYPES OF CLIMBING VINES

Twining

A twining vine is one of God's many miracles. The stems and sometimes the new leaves of these types of vines sense a "guide" and will twirl around that guide. The most important thing to remember when planting a twiner is that it will need a trellis or pole with a small circumference to get started. A large trellis with big slats is too flat and wide for a small vine to start twining around. You can "lead" a vine to a larger trellis by providing small poles to twine around initially. Twiners include beans, morning glories, wisteria, jasmine and honeysuckle. All of these vines can go a little crazy if you are not careful with them. Make certain to keep them in check by pruning or separating them in a section of the garden where they will not take over smaller, more delicate plants.

Rambling

Rambling vines are the type that seem to tumble over everything in sight. They have a vining look, but not a vining habit. In other words, they cannot climb. These plants need to be attached or placed onto a trellis, arbor or established tree in order to thrive. Once laid out on a guide, they must be attached via twine or loosely looped twist ties. Climbing roses are the most notable plant in this category, while blackberries and raspberries can also be considered ramblers.

Tendrils

Tendrils are the classic attachment device of the pea. Shooting out from the stem like miniature arms, the tendrils grab onto guides and hold onto them for dear life like a newborn baby's clutch. Sweet peas, edible peas and the entire family of grapes attach via tendrils. Make sure you give tendrils a place to hold onto or they will hold onto each other creating a mass of plants that do not produce particularly well. Small circumference guides are a must for this group of vines, and they will do best with a "mesh"-type product to grow up and out on.

Sticky Vines

I put both adhesive pads and aerial rootlets in this group. These are the vines that attach via "hairy" roots or little pads that leave marks all over your siding when you pull them off. There is not a whole lot you need to know about caring for this group because they will often care for themselves. The ivies, creepers and climbing hydrangea all grow in this manner. The most important thing you need to know is that they can *eat your house* or any structure or plant they come near. We have masses of ivy growing around our home and woods, but it is growing on stone and massive established trees. Be careful growing sticky vines on siding, wooden structures and young plants. They can do serious damage. That said, this plant group can be fantastic for indoor plant arrangements where you need a tough and hardy climber. Clematis has a long shot at surviving indoors, but an English ivy will do just fine.

Once you have figured out which type of vine you are dealing with and have given it a proper guiding or staking, it is time to offer it a little food and water. Aside from roses, which are heavy feeders, vines honestly don't need much. In general, they are not fussy and if you pick a vine that is known to do well in your region, typical rainfall and a bit of compost throughout the season should feed them just fine.

While there are plenty of vines to choose from, I am going to share two of my favorites with you. They are both fantastic for providing fast and easy fruit, but can both also be used in crafting. Let's start with the blackberries, shall we?

GROWING BLACKBERRIES

Berries are a great climber choice for home gardeners because they will provide fruit by their second or third year and sometimes even in their first year. Compare that to a fruit *tree* that takes anywhere from 4 to 7 years to start producing its first crop of fruit. The typical problem with fruit caning plants however, is the thorns. Enter blackberries. There are plenty of thornless varieties of blackberries, making them hands down my favorite berry to grow.

Start with a small plant from your local nursery or a cutting from a friend. Blackberries grow quickly, so there is little need to buy large plants. To root a cutting, simply dip in rooting hormone and place directly into the ground with 2 inches (5 cm) underground. If you have a mature blackberry plant, you can "layer" canes to make new plants. Simply pull a cane down towards the ground, cover with a small mound of soil and a stone to weigh it down. By the next spring, that piece will have rooted and you will have a new plant! The blackberry plant often completes this layering process on its own as a natural propagation.

Berries are supposed to have full sun, but I have had them growing successfully in almost every type of partial sun/shade environment in my garden. In partial shade, they will not produce as many berries, but they grow enough for casual garden picking and also provide tons of crafting vines. The canes will ramble in and through established evergreens and other perennials. The canes can also be attached to a trellis or arbor. The more you prune your blackberries, the more fruit they will put out. Just make sure you do not prune more than half the plant at one time.

Here are a few of my favorite thornless varieties.

Navajo
This old school thornless blackberry is the one I grow in my garden and have propagated many times. The fruit has a tart start but ends sweet and it propagates very, very well. The patent on this particular plant has expired, making it a perfect plant for a self-propagated hedge via one starter plant.

Prime-Ark-Freedom
From the University of Arkansas, new at Burpee in 2015, this thornless blackberry is the first primocane-fruiting blackberry. That means you can get a first year summer harvest as well as a fall harvest. This blackberry is under patent, so you will not want to propagate it yet!

Triple-Crown
Also from Burpee, this thornless blackberry is known for its sweetness and masses of berries.

GROWING GRAPEVINES

Unlike the blackberries, which need a little help finding a home to ramble upon, grapevines will reach out via tendrils and pull themselves up and around an arbor. In my previous garden, I grew Concord grapes up three sides of a large room arbor, training the vines to climb up to the top and over to meet each other. If we had stayed in our home a few more years, I would have been able to pick those grapes hanging down from the "ceiling." How delightful! Grapevines take a bit longer to become established than blackberries, and they also require more vigorous pruning to keep them moving in the direction you would like them to go. All that pruning results in fantastic crafting materials, especially during the years you wait for the grapes to be ready for harvest.

To get started, you will want to either buy a plant from your local nursery or take cuttings from a mature plant. My favorite time to take cuttings is in summer when the plant will still have green growth, but the vines are strong. Take 3 to 4 inch (7 to 10 cm) cuttings, dip in rooting hormone and place in a pot with growing medium. The cuttings will start rooting in 2 to 4 weeks and can be planted out in fall. Alternatively, hardwood cuttings can be taken in late fall, dipped in rooting hormone and placed into a pot with growing medium. They will take many weeks, perhaps the whole winter, to sprout.

CREATE YOUR OWN GRAPEVINE TRELLISES, TREES, WREATHS AND DÉCOR

When pruning, take off pieces of straight cane that are as long as possible to create wreaths and trellises. Small pieces will also be useful, but you need a foundation of older, straight canes. Once pruned, bend the flexible canes into shapes before drying. You see, the grapevines and the blackberry canes will bend easily while green, but once dry and brown, they are fairly strong and stiff. This is the exact characteristic that makes them perfect for wreath bases! Secure vines with garden twine or natural colored twist ties and allow them to dry in a cool dark place. Consider spraying them with a protective spray if you plan to use them outdoors. Even without spraying, a vine wreath or trellis will last several seasons in the garden. Here are a few of my favorite shapes!

THE BASIC WREATH

Attach 3 to 4 long canes together with twine and twist into a rounded curve. Add in 2 to 4 canes every few inches, securing with each new bunch. Once the wreath is full and round, dry in a cool dark space

VINE BALLS

The easiest way to create these little balls is to use a balloon. Simply blow up a balloon to the size you prefer and wrap medium, flexible vines around the balloon, securing when necessary with twist ties or small vines. The tendrils and vines will start to "catch" on each other as you wrap around and around. Allow the ball to dry with the balloon intact and then puncture the balloon once the ball is fully cured.

VINE STARS

This classic shape is made by creating a basic star out of small, thick canes and then wrapping it in small bits to create a 3D shape.

FUN SHAPES

Large vines can provide strong outlines while small vines can provide pretty details. To create intricate shapes, draw a design on paper and then place the vines atop the paper while building. Secure with strong, natural colored twist ties and allow to dry before hanging.

GRAPEVINE "TREES" OR TOWERS"

Cut 3 to 6 strong, thick canes to the same length. Place in a teepee shape and secure at the top via twine or another vine. Wrap smaller vines loosely around this base. Allow to cure in a cool, dry place.

BAUBLES AND BITS

I like using my grapevine forms as they are, enjoying their natural form, but they can definitely serve as a base for more elaborate presentations. Small flowers can be woven into the trees; wreaths, stars and ribbons can be knotted onto wreaths for pretty fairy circles!

Vine balls work well for indoor décor and garden decoration.

Wrap vines around a twig base to create various shapes (pictured: star).

VINE BASKET

To create a basket, start with large vines and wrap in a circle, stacking them on top of each other. Secure with wire. Take smaller grapevines and continue wrapping, tucking vines under protruding pieces, until the basket is full. Wrap wire vertically around the entire piece. Add a handle if you wish! Once your "basket" is complete, simply place a pot inside with flowers overflowing for a beautiful planted look!

PRACTICAL VINE SHAPES

Last year at Christmastime, I was trying to hang a wreath onto a stone bridge, but had no tools along with me. The solution? A vine. I grabbed a piece of ivy, wrapped it around the wreath and a bridge light and voila! As it dried, the vine strengthened into shape and the wreath hung all winter. Consider this natural material when making all manner of practical devices in the garden. Your options might include:

1. Rope for attaching plants to trellises or wreaths to structures

2. The basis for a wattle fencing around the vegetable garden

3. Small vine circles as "hooks" (see vine star on page 33)

4. Half-circle vine balls to cushion and hold large pumpkins or squash off the ground

5. Baskets for harvesting fruits and vegetables

6. Rope substitute for any manner of chores!

AMY'S RED, WHITE AND BLUE JAM

The start of summer means the start of berry season and if you are lucky, you will be harvesting these fruits even earlier in the season. Get them quick, or else the bunnies and birdies will have a field day with them! Now, there are two camps when it comes to berry preserves: the jam lovers and the jelly lovers. I happen to be a jam type of girl, so that is the method I will share with you today. Jelly, however, is similar, just minus all the berry chunk goodness. This particular recipe uses the tart, distinctive taste of lime in place of traditional lemon. Feel free to substitute a traditional lemon or experiment with other citrus. The citrus provides natural pectin to the jam, but I have also included powdered pectin for a strong set jam. Also note that this is a small recipe. Jams, particularly for beginners, do best in small batches!

YIELD—TWO 8-OZ (237-ML) JARS

1 large lime or 2 small Key limes

2 cups (400 g) white sugar

½ cup (76 g) strawberries, hulled and quartered

½ cup (61 g) raspberries

½ cup (74 g) blueberries

½ cup (72 g) blackberries

3 tbsp (44 ml) quick set pectin

¼ tsp almond extract

1. Sterilize canning jars, rinse and dry.

2. Zest and juice the lime into a medium sized bowl with the sugar.

3. Add all the berries and pectin. Stir and mash the mixture for 5 minutes or until mixture is mostly smooth, with some small chunks remaining.

4. Allow the mixture to rest for 5 to 10 minutes, then stir and mash for another minute or so.

5. Decant into canning jars and enjoy! The jam can be preserved using traditional pressure-canning methods, used up immediately (yum!) or frozen once cooled. I will be honest—our jams don't last into winter and are usually eaten up within a week of being made!

Mash berry mixture until only small fruit chunks remain.

DID YOU KNOW? Frozen fruit can be substituted for any fresh fruits in these recipes. Frozen fruit is often picked at the peak of freshness and instantly frozen, so it can actually be fresher than the berries at the grocery store! However, nothing beats fresh out of the backyard garden, especially those blackberry vines you learned how to grow in the beginning of the chapter!

DID YOU KNOW? You can save your lemon seeds for a natural pectin boost for jams. Just keep them in a little bag in the freezer and break them out while jam making. Simply bundle all the seeds in a little cheesecloth and add to the simmering jam for a hit of pectin! Note that the lemon seeds replace pectin, not lemon juice or zest in a recipe.

CLASSIC GRAPE JELLY

Cool fall days and lingering dark nights signal plants to put on their last fruit-filled show. They produce as much as possible to ensure plenty of seeds for the next generation. For humans, this means we eat like kings. When grapes, blackberries and all manner of annuals are providing a first or second flush of fruit, it is time to get jelly making! Gather up as many bushels as you can and jump into the kitchen for some delicious and beautiful jewel-toned jellies.

YIELD—THREE 8-OZ (237-ML) JARS

2 lbs (908 g) purple grapes

¾ cup (177 ml) water

½ to 1 cup (100 to 200 g) sugar

2 tbsp (29 ml) classic pectin

1. Sterilize canning jars, rinse and dry.

2. Since we are making jelly, not jam, we need to extract the juice from the grapes. To do this, wash the grapes and place them in a large stock pot with ¾ cup (117 ml) of water. Cook on low heat until they start to break down, about 15 to 20 minutes.

3. Strain the juice from the solids with a colander and large pot or applesauce sieve. You should end up with about 2 cups (473 ml) of juice.

4. Add the sugar to your stockpot of grape juice. Use ½ cup to 1 cup (100 to 200 g) depending on how sweet you want it. This recipe is a low sugar option. Commercial jellies and traditional recipes will have up to 3 to 4 cups (600 to 800 g) of sugar for this size batch.

5. Continue cooking on low and add pectin, stirring often. After 15 to 20 minutes, test to see if a drop of jelly sets up on a frozen plate or chilled glass. Continue cooking if it is still too wet.

6. When a drop of jelly slightly solidifies on the frozen plate or chilled glass, it is ready to pour! Decant into canning jars immediately.

7. The jam can be preserved using traditional pressure-canning methods, used up immediately (yum!) or frozen once cooled. If you have concerns over the safety of canning your own condiments, freezing is a great option that does not require a full seal on jars. Simply decant the jelly into jars, cool and place into the freezer. Once opened, store in the refrigerator for 2 to 3 weeks. Frozen jams and jellies will last up to a year or longer.

Concord grapes ripening on an iron arbor.

NOTE: Try serving up this jelly with some hot toasted peanut butter toast! I first had this treat on our way home from six months in Thailand. Six months with no peanut butter and they were serving hot toast with good old American peanut butter and jelly on top at a food stand in the Bangkok airport. Eating regular cold PB&J was never the same.

section two

GATHERED ON A WOODLAND WALK

Crackling bonfires, a crisp bite in the air and dive-bombing acorns are all signs of the fall of the garden. Sweater weather, football games and the closing of the garden are the seasonal rites of fall. While closing the garden is somewhat melancholy, it also signals a time of rest for the gardener. That last about two weeks and then the gardening crafters are hungry for something to do with their hands and their creative minds. Well, the woods will oblige and provide buckets and baskets of crafting materials ripe for collecting and crafting.

In these two chapters, we will focus on the cones and the corns and then the twigs and branches. We will dive into responsibly caring for the future of the woods, while still enjoying a bountiful harvest of supplies. There is plenty for us *and* the squirrels! Join me as we break out the wood burning and sawing tools, wax and even a little yarn for a simple knit piece accented with handmade wooden buttons!

CHAPTER 4

GATHERING CONES & CORNS
FOR FALL CRAFTING

Walk into the forest and before long, you are bound to hear that distinctive *crunch* as you step on a pinecone. They are everywhere in evergreen forests and free for the taking! As always, leave some to keep the natural order, but in a mature forest, there are always more than enough pinecones. They would never all grow into full sized trees under a mature canopy, so feel free to gather your free crafting supplies without guilt! Once gathered, those buckets of pinecones, acorns, seed pods and nuts make fantastic additions to your craft closet!

HOW TO GATHER AND PREPARE CONES FOR CRAFTING

There are a few things you must know before gathering pinecones. First and foremost, beware the "sticky"! Every pinecone comes complete with "pitch," the sticky sap that the females use to reproduce. The female pinecones are the ones you are familiar with and vary slightly from species to species. The male cone produces pollen and is relatively the same across various pine species. Think of the female pinecone as one of those women who just seem to draw men to them like flies to honey. The cone secretes sticky sap that literally captures the male pollen when blown by the wind. Pretty fantastic, right?

The second thing to note before gathering pinecones is that some will be wet and closed, while others will be dry and open. Did you know that pinecones actually open and close based on moisture levels many times during their life cycle? In fact, the prevalence of open or dry cones can be used to gauge how wet the forest is and how likely forest fires are. As a crafter, you can use wet or dry cones, but you must use them differently. Traditionally, dry and open cones are desired, but I think the green or wet cones can be quite beautiful as table décor or wreath accents.

Thirdly, pinecones can sometimes be the homes of small critters and undesirable pests. Beware. Are you a little petrified of picking up a pinecone now? Don't be! Get your gloves on and get hiking! Bring along a bucket or bag to collect the cones. Collect a variety of sizes, and experiment with both wet and dry cones. You might want a sticky/wet bucket and a dry bucket if collecting various types.

WHICH SPECIES SHOULD I COLLECT? WHICH ARE BEST FOR CRAFTING?

When hunting down pinecones, you might not be able to find the exact species that I am using in these crafts. Note that any open/dry cone can be substituted for the cones I am using in the following crafts. Here is a quick rundown for you of the various types you might find on your woodland walk.

Pinecones
The most traditional cone that you are probably familiar with is the cone from pine trees. Longleaf Pine cones and Shortleaf Pine cones look very similar, but differ vastly in size. The Slash pine cone has a beautiful shape, perfect for crafting. Ponderosa Pines have a beautiful pointed shape to them, making them darling miniature Christmas trees, shown at their best when flecked with artificial snow.

Fir Cones
Fir cones have an elongated shape that makes them ideal for making pinecone totems, stick figures or beautiful spiked wreaths. When disassembled, the dry scales of Fir cones make beautiful flowers and designs.

Spruce Cones
Spruce cones are long and narrow, the darling of the cones. The shape is beautiful for Christmas garlands or accenting wreaths. Colorado spruce scales are slightly spikier than other spruces, making them good for little trees in a fairy garden. I love the green cones of a white spruce. Elongated and a brilliant fresh green, these cones are great for non-traditional Christmas decorating.

Hemlock Cones
Hemlock cones are some of my favorites, but are not as easily found as the common pine cones are. They are short and flower-like, with large scales that look like petals. These make darling mini-firestarters, tiny peanut butter laced birdfeeders or accents for any number of crafts. If you find hemlock cones, you are a lucky crafter indeed!

Once your pinecones are collected, you need to combat that sticky pitch and pesky critters. My favorite method is to line a large roasting pan with foil and lay the mostly dry pinecones in a layer. Bake at 200°F (93°C) for 20 minutes and the pitch will glaze the pinecones, giving a nice glazed finish to the cone. This baking also takes care of any pests. Wet pinecones can be washed with a generous amount of soap, but will still maintain a slight bit of stickiness. If your hands are sticky from messing with the cones, wash them as usual and then scrub with coconut or olive oil under water. Gently towel dry. The oil will help remove any residual stickiness and also give your hands a nice moisturizing treatment.

WHAT ABOUT THE ACORNS?

Where pines and spruce abound, you are also likely to find an oak tree or two. In fact, walk around in the fall on a windy day, and chances are an acorn or two will pelt you over the head. While oak is a fantastic wood for crafting furniture, I think its real charm is in its acorns. Collecting acorns is a slightly different experience from cone hunting in that they are food for woodland inhabitants. In fact, the acorn nut itself was once food for the Native Americans and today artisans collect acorns and create flour, roasted nuts and other products in today's gourmet marketplace. Note that if you wish to eat the acorn nuts, you must soak them to remove the tannin. They are not edible by humans without this step. Squirrels, however, simply hole them up in trees for the winter and the snow and ice naturally remove the tannin.

Thus, while collecting acorns, consider leaving the actual nuts and collecting only the beautiful acorn caps for crafting. While taking a few acorn nuts here and there will do no harm, collecting all of the nuts in a given area might spell disaster for the resident chipmunks' winter diet.

TYPES OF ACORNS

There are various sizes and shapes of acorns and they can be collected green or brown. Green acorns are still "wet" and usually still hanging on the tree. They are not ready to eat, but do look adorable for crafting. Brown acorn nuts have almost always fallen from the tree, are ready to collect and process for eating and will often be separated from their caps. I collect as many caps as I can and collect only "full acorns" when I choose to use them with the nuts intact.

> » **Willow Oak.** These acorns are super tiny and seem to be perfectly proportioned for acorn heads and fairy gardens.

> » **Scarlet Oak and Northern Red Oak.** Fat and jolly, these acorns are gorgeous as part of garlands for fall.

> » **Northern Pine Oak**. These medium-sized acorn caps are great for multi-purpose crafting.

> » **Bur Oak.** Also fat, but furry, are the Bur Oak acorns, which include a frilly finish on each acorn cap. Could there be any more perfect topper for an acorn peg person?

> » **Live Oak and Oregon White Oak.** These acorns have a beautiful elongated shape, though very different colors. The Live Oaks are a deep and beautiful brown with crimson undertones while the White Oaks are a typical light brown.

Like the cones, once you bring the acorns inside, give them a short bake at 200°F (93°C) for 15 to 20 minutes to make sure no critters take a ride inside on your crafting supplies.

Acorns must be leached with water, then cracked and ground before eating.

DIY FIRESTARTER CONE CUPCAKES

Arguably my favorite cone craft is the beautiful, yet incredibly functional firestarter. These make fantastic gifts for a host with a functional fireplace or Christmas gifts for friends who go camping or enjoy backyard fire-pit parties. If your family enjoys camping and s'mores, you could create a whole basket of these fun cone firestarters!

YIELD—10 FIRESTARTERS

(continued)

DIY FIRE STARTER CONE CUPCAKES (CONTINUED)

10 small dry pinecones with wide, open scales

1 lb (454 g) slab of beeswax or paraffin wax (or leftover wax from candles)

Small melting crockpot, double boiler or microwave-safe bowl

Thick paper cupcake wrappers

1 to 2 cups (around 100 g) sawdust (*not* from pre-treated wood)

1. Prep your pinecones by baking at 200°F (93°C) for 20 minutes or until sap has glazed the pinecones. Smaller pinecones will take less time than the larger ones.

2. While the pinecones are being prepped, melt your wax in small 3 to 4 inch (7.5 to 10 cm) pieces in a small crockpot on low. Alternatively, melt old candles on a candle warmer.

3. Fill each cupcake wrapper half full with sawdust. *Do not* use sawdust from pre-treated wood due to chemicals.

4. Gently pour melted wax over the sawdust until it just covers the sawdust, about halfway up the cupcake wrapper.

5. Add another small layer of melted wax and immediately push a small pinecone into the cupcake as far as it will go. Gently pour wax over the pinecone scales, keeping the very tip wax free.

6. Allow the cupcakes to fully harden and store right side up. Do not remove from paper cupcake wrapper.

7. To use, light the top of the pinecone and the side of the paper wrapper. The fire will slowly and steadily start and wax will evaporate as traditional candles do. Fire should always be contained in a fire pit or fireplace.

Beware that pinecones can sometimes "pop" a bit while burning—keep back!

FAIRY SCONCES

Often, acorns grow several caps to a branch and fall in one piece. When two caps fall together at a right angle, they make the perfect fairy sconce. A fairy sconce is a cheap and easy way to add a little faux lighting to your fairy garden (see page 15) or add a bit of whimsy to a tree in your garden.

Two acorn caps joined at a right angle

Marble

Glue

1. Wash and dry (or bake) your acorn caps to make sure they are free of pest eggs.

2. Make sure the two acorns are at a right angle by placing one against a flat surface and noting whether the second hangs directly out from the wall at a 90° angle.

3. Attach a marble to the extended acorn cap with hot glue or regular glue (for kids).

4. "Install" your fairy sconces in a fairy house or directly onto a tree via super glue on a dry day. Wet bark will not accept glue.

NOTE: These decorations will last a few weeks, or at best a full season, outdoors. Indoors, they will last much longer!

MINI MUSHROOMS

This little project is a darling addition to fairy gardens, and is simple enough that very young children can participate! For speed, use a hot glue gun, but for children, opt for regular white glue or craft glue.

Acorn caps

Small twigs

Hot glue or regular school glue

1. Wash and dry (or bake) your acorn caps and twigs to make sure they are free of pest eggs.

2. Cut twigs to lengths between 2 to 4 inches (5 to 10 cm) long.

3. Glue acorn caps directly atop twigs, putting a drop of glue into the cap first and placing the twig down onto the cap.

4. Allow the "mushrooms" to dry upside down, with the cap portion resting on parchment paper or foil.

5. Use the little mushrooms in fairy gardens or to create a little field of mushrooms in a secluded place in the backyard. Your children have the imagination to make this craft spark hours of play.

"ACORN HEADS" PEG PEOPLE

Acorn caps make great hats for tiny peg or stick people. A little hot glue and a little imagination will help you create toys that your kids can play with for hours. Get the kids involved in the project from start to finish, gathering acorns, choosing outfits, gluing hair and even building homes for their acorn heads!

YIELD—20 PEG PEOPLE

20 wooden pegs and/or old-fashioned clothespins

Various bits of fabric, yarn and odds and ends to decorate

Glue

20 acorn caps

Floral tape (optional)

Markers, watercolor pencils and/or paint

1. Start with a basic peg or old-fashioned clothespin and add a little yarn or string for hair with a hot glue gun.

2. Once dry, attach an acorn top as a small little "cap."

3. Wind floral tape around the body of the doll or simply use paints or fabric bits to create outfits for your dolls.

4. Draw little faces with watercolor pencils or paint or leave blank.

5. Add your acorn heads to a dollhouse, place in fairy gardens or hide as little surprises in the veggie garden!

NOTE: If you don't have wooden pegs or clothespins to spare, you can make acorn head people with just acorns and twigs! Simply gather acorns with the caps attached and an equal number of small branches or twigs, about half an inch (1 cm) thick. The branch circumference should be about the same size as the acorn nut, and should be cut straight across for a clean line. Glue the acorn nut onto the cut branch, and adorn like the peg people.

"Faceless" dolls are beautifully simple and reminiscent of Amish or Mennonite dolls.

EASY WOODLAND SCENT POTS

This is perhaps the easiest project in this book, requiring simple supplies and a quick woodland hike to collect the acorns, branches, nut hulls and pinecones needed. If you are intimidated by essential oils, soap-making and natural crafting in general, a scent pot is a fantastic place to start! Scent pots are simply containers of natural materials that are able to soak up the rich, layered scents of essential oils and return that scent back into a space little bit by bit. Turning the materials in the scent pot with a spoon or warming the scent pot will release even stronger scents.

Wood gatherings, such as nut hulls, acorns, dry branch bits, etc.

Container (I used a metal bucket, but you can use any cute container you might have or find in a thrift store)

Orchid moss (available at any garden center or nursery, found on clearance in late summer)

Essential oils of your choice (clary sage and bergamot are a nice mix)

1. Make sure *all* of your supplies are completely clean and dry. That means cleaning all woodland bits and your container in hot, soapy water and allowing them to dry for a day or so. The orchid moss is fine straight out of the package.

2. If you are using a large container that has more space than you have filler, you can use plastic packaging or even bubble wrap to fill the space. Cover with orchid moss and then layer your beautiful acorns and such on top.

3. Sprinkle 40 to 50 drops of essential oil onto the top of your mix, dropping the oil onto the orchid moss, rather than the twigs and bark. While dry woodland bits *will* accept scent, the orchid moss does a much better job. Note that I used a combination of clary sage and bergamot for a nice "earthy" scent, but you can use whatever oil scent appeals to you!

4. Place your finished bucket of woodland scents wherever you need a little pick-me-up and refresh with additional oil when the scent fades after a few months.

NOTE: I use orchid moss on top of many of my indoor potted plants because it looks attractive and can be found for pennies at the end of the growing season. The stores need room for Christmas-Christmas-Christmas, so anything garden gets clearanced out fast! I buy anything I need that will last at that time. Tools, potting soil, pots, fertilizer and more! I use much of it for my indoor garden, but most will last through until spring as well. If you get ahead of the game, there is no reason to pay full retail prices in spring. Look through the gardening section with an eye open for supplies that can be used for crafting as well as gardening. Pretty accessories, tools and some planting materials fit the bill. The orchid moss in this "recipe" absorbs the oils even better than your little woodland "bits" and blends into the bottom of your container. You can do this project without it, but your scent pot will stay fragrant much longer with it!

CHAPTER 5

GATHERING TWIGS & BRANCHES FOR WOODLAND CRAFTS

When you walk through a forest, you are bound to see plenty of fallen trees, snapped twigs and cracked branches. While some larger logs might provide essential habitats for animals, most of the crafting sized wood pieces are free for the taking. Pruning off broken branches and clearing a stream of twigs can actually be quite beneficial to the wildlife and environment. In this chapter, I give you a few tips for gathering responsibly and then we dive into some fun crafts like making wooden buttons for a pretty loom hat and burning your own wooden coin magnets.

DO'S AND DON'TS FOR WOODLAND GATHERING

We have already discussed a few of the do's and don'ts of woodland gathering in Chapter 4, namely leaving plenty of materials and food for both the woodland creatures and the botanical future of the woods. There are a few more tips that are important when gathering twigs and branches from the woods. Here is what you need to know.

Always consider the life cycle of the plant you are collecting from. There are seasons when plants are at their most fragile and you can kill them by cutting off too many branches. For example, pruning a rosebush right at the start of winter will force it to put on new growth and if a freeze comes along, your rosebush is dead.

Consider how much of the plant you are taking. An old, established tree can take a few branches pruned at any time, but that same amount from a young plant might spell its doom.

Consider the age of the plant's roots. You have already considered whether the plant is old or young, but what about the age of its roots? If you recently moved the tree into a new location, the roots might not have had time to become established. Pruning a tree puts stress on it and if the roots cannot give the tree enough water and nutrients to thrive, a pruning could do it in.

Are you gathering branches from a flowering bush or tree? Gathering while it's in flower is rarely a problem unless you take more than a third of the plant. However, if you gather tons of branches in winter from a flowering bush, the flower show in spring will be terrible. Many flowering trees set their flower buds in the fall and winter for the next spring. Don't prune them in the winter unless you are pruning to force blooms.

Are you simply collecting twigs and branches from the woodland floor? Good for you! Typically, branches that have fallen to the woodland floor are a great choice for collecting, but beware pest eggs and other critters coming inside with the twigs. Wash and bake at 200°F (93°C) for 15 to 20 minutes to be safe. Also, be careful collecting from creek banks or large logs. These might provide habitats for woodland creatures or help prevent erosion of the creek banks. Feel free to use the woods, but be conscious of what you are taking and what effect it might have.

Wood-burned slices make great magnets, keychains or ornaments!

HOW TO MAKE WOODEN BUTTONS

Wooden buttons are charming and can fit a range of styles. While wooden buttons can be purchased, I find it far more satisfying to make them instead! A few simple tools and supplies are all you need, along with a bit of time whittling away while the snow and ice rage outside. Light a pine and nutmeg candle, get the Christmas music cranking and this activity can be quite delightful.

Dremel or small saw to cut wood coins

Wood coins, cut from a fresh or newly fallen branch, roughly 1 inch (2.5 cm) wide and ¼ inch (0.6 cm) thick or smaller

Dremel, wood burning tool or small drill to make holes

Wood carving tools for optional decoration

1. You want to use fresh wood or newly fallen wood for buttons so that you are not dealing with wet and rotting wood. After cutting the wood coins, allow them to dry out for a few days before carving or bake at a very low temperature (about 200°F [93°C]) for 15 minutes.

2. Use a Dremel or small drill to place 1, 2 or 4 holes in the middle of your button for a traditional button. You could certainly also make 3, 6 or 8 holes and try a new looping technique to attach your buttons.

3. Add accents to your button by carving the edges or adding designs with a wood burning tool to the face of the button.

4 Attach your new button to knitwear, gift packaging, floral wraps or other crafting projects!

Drill buttonholes with a manual drill.

Little wooden buttons can accessorize hats, scarves and sweaters.

LOOM KNIT A SLOUCH HAT WITH WOODEN BUTTON ACCENTS

Loom knitting is a fun new way to dip your toes into the world of textiles without much experience or skill. It takes a few tries to really get going, but the learning curve is much lower than with traditional knitting. In other words, anyone can do it!

You can create beanies, infinity scarves, tiny baby hats, boot cuffs, neck warmers, mug cozies and more with a circle loom. You simply need comfy, cozy yarn, a round loom and one basic "picking" tool. The kit I use came with four sizes of looms, allowing plenty of room for experimenting with different sizes. My favorite project thus far with my looms is a slouch hat that fits just right for winter. This project takes 2 to 3 hours to complete once you get the hang of the technique.

(continued)

LOOM KNIT A SLOUCH HAT WITH WOODEN BUTTON ACCENTS (CONTINUED)

Yarn

Circle loom

Pick

Wooden Buttons (page 54, optional)

1. Choose a nice, soft, luxurious yarn. Spend a little bit of money here, because it matters significantly to the end project. I like Lion Brand "Homespun" from Consumer Crafts. It costs 5 to 6 dollars per skein, and is the softest yarn I have found at the lowest price. A small baby hat will take half a skein while a slouch hat or infinity scarf will take one to two skeins depending on how large you make it.

2. Loop the end of your yarn around the little "peg" on the side of the circle loom to secure it. That peg simply acts as a second hand to keep the yarn steady while you work.

3. Start looping your yarn around each peg of the circle, making a loose round. Work clockwise or counter clockwise and keep going the same direction for the entire project.

4. Once you complete one circle around, do another right on top, so that each peg has two loops around it.

5. Using a pick, grab the bottom loop and pull it up over the second yarn loop, over the peg and off of the loom towards the center of the loom. Continue with each peg around the circle and you have completed one line. Continue making two loops around, then pulling the bottom layer up and off with your pick.

6. To finish a hat, I find it works best to knot each final loop for security. Once you have knit a 12- to 16-inch (30- to 40-cm) set of lines and are down to *one* layer of loops on your circle loom, begin taking them off one at a time, knotting them to your end thread and pulling tightly to create the top of your hat.

7. Add wooden buttons or other decorations to your loomed slouch hat!

THE BASICS OF WOOD BURNING

Wood burning, or pyrography, is a skill that starts out very simply with elementary strokes, but can become very complex as your skill increases. Choose a wood like pine that is "soft" and burns easily. Here are a few basics to get you started!

STRAIGHT LINE

Hold the carving tool at an angle on the wood, allowing it to burn into the wood before moving. Move slowly, with a consistent pressure on the tool to create a straight, grooved line. Your speed will have more of an impact on the depth of the line than the pressure, but steady, strong pressure helps keep the tool straight.

CURVED LINES

Draw out curved lines prior to burning them and follow along the line at a 45° angle with a medium pressure on the tool. A heavy pressure will cause the tool to "skid" across the wood, ruining your line, while light pressure will not make enough of an impact.

DOTS

Use the sharp or pointed attachment or side of the tool and press straight down onto the wood to make dots.

EYES

To create slightly slanted eyes, use the same technique as dots, but angle the tool slightly, holding for 3 to 4 seconds for the main part of the eye, then gently pulling away at an angle to create the slant of an eye.

SCRAPED

Turned on its side, a wood-burning tool can make really beautiful scrapes to fill in clothing, provide waves in an ocean or add movement to a sky. Think of the tool as a piece of chalk used on its side. Turned almost horizontal with your piece of wood, the tool drags across the wood with medium pressure creating a thick "scrape."

TREE BRANCHES

For any light, wispy type of lines, you need to use a light pressure and quick speed. Once you have used straight and curved lines to set a frame for your picture, add in wispy lines to create texture and movement with an angled tool.

To draw a curved line with a wood-burning tool, use a 45° angle.

WOOD-BURNED ABC MAGNETS

If you are anything like me, it drives me bananas to have bright pink and blue and florescent green alphabet letters on my fridge. The solution? Pretty carved wooden ABC letters! Join me as I show you how to make your own! These ABC magnets look beautiful and rustic on the fridge, and can be arranged to spell out fun or inspiring words.

2 to 3 wooden branches about 1- to 2-inches (2.5- to 5-cm) in diameter

Manual or power saw

Wood-burning tool

Magnet strips and scissors or heavy duty round magnets

Hot glue and hot glue gun

1. Cut the branches into coins that are about a ½-inch (1.3-cm) thick. Thicker coins will have too much weight for the magnets to hold them.

2. Use a wood-burning tool to carve the letters and numbers into the wood.

3. Attach magnet tape to the back of each coin with hot glue and allow to cool upside down on a flat surface. It is best to use hot glue as opposed to a self-adhesive magnet for more staying power. Some heavy-duty magnets might be strong enough, but I have had good luck with hot glue.

4. Once dry, the magnets are ready to go on the fridge. Let the learning begin!

NOTE: Don't feel limited to only making alphabet magnets! You can also write full words, create pretty designs or draw little pictures. The wooden coins can be strung with hemp for ornaments, hung as a garland or used as a personalized gift topper. The possibilities are endless! Let your creativity run wild!

Use a wood-burning tool to create cute ABC magnets.

section three

GATHERED FROM YOUR PANTRY

Humble. Common. Cheap. Dirty roots. You don't think I am being derogatory, now do you? Those words signify a special place I have in my heart for the root vegetables of the world—particularly the potato, the onion, the beet and the ginger root. They all make incredible crafting materials and can be found for pennies on the dollar at your local grocery store. They are all also incredibly easy to grow in a backyard garden. Of course, the quality of your crop will depend on the quality of your soil, but I hasten to say that any average Joe can plant an onion set or some beet seed and at the very least get beet greens and green onions!

In this section, we use these common root vegetables in uncommon ways: for dyes and stamps, flowers and wreaths. The skins, greens and the roots are all used. What is typically trash can be crafting gold.

CHAPTER 6

FROM YOUR PANTRY—BEET TOPS

You might immediately associate the word "beet" with slices of congealed, vinegar-laden salad bar accoutrements, but they can be so much more. In fact, you might just skip the traditional red flesh all together in favor of growing beet greens or using beet's natural dye. Beets contain one of the most vivid natural dyes available and lucky for us, beets are cheap and easy to grow!

HOW TO GROW BEETS (AND WHY YOU WOULD *WANT* TO!)

Beets grow very well from seed and are readily available and inexpensive. Simply sprinkle seeds on the surface of a pot of rich potting soil and water them in gently. When planting seeds, you will want to use a watering can with a "rose" that breaks the water stream into gentle trickles. Keep soil moist but not wet until the seeds sprout.

If you are growing beets for the root, thin seedlings to a spacing of 3 to 5 inches (7.6 to 12.6 cm) apart by cutting seedlings at the soil line with small scissors. (I know! This part is terrifying!) However, if you are growing beets for the greens, you can keep many more plants in one small space. They don't need that same room to stretch out and grow under the soil, so as long as you are growing them in a rich potting soil, many plants can survive and thrive.

HOW TO GROW BEETS FROM BEET TOPS

Let's stop for a moment and consider another method, shall we? Growing beets from seed *is* rather easy, but there is another way that is arguably more fun. Grab up some cheap beets from the "seconds" stand of your local market. It is okay if they are looking a little beat up. We are going to cut off those sad looking parts anyway.

1. Chop the leaves off of the beets with about 1 to 2 inches (2.5 to 5 cm) of green still attached to the beet.

2. Slice the beet root about one inch from the top. Peel and roast the bottom portion of the beet with olive oil, salt and pepper in a 350°F (177°C) oven until fork tender. *Save the peels* for beet dye.

3. Here is the fun part! Place those little beet tops in a glass vessel and fill with water just to the point where the stem begins to grow from the root. The beets will float slightly, but tend to keep their roots submerged. I have success with several plants nestled together in a container to help keep them upright. (See photo.)

4. The beets will almost instantly start coloring the water a beautiful shade of crimson. Let them sit in the water and refresh when the water level decreases. I tend to leave mine sitting next to the kitchen sink where they receive indirect sunlight. Note that if you are attempting to grow beet *roots* for consumption, you will need full sun and rich soil, but beet greens are much less picky.

5. The leaves will start to grow again and tiny white water roots will begin to grow from the bottom. Those fresh, new baby beet leaves are perfect for green smoothies and salads. Packed chock full of nutrition and adding a slight sweetness typical to kales and such, the beet green is such a happy addition to your arsenal!

You might be surprised to note that the water in the glass will start to turn back to clear after a few hours. If you want beet dye, you will need to take the first water from your cuttings or use only the peels you saved earlier. Use it or lose it baby!

DID YOU KNOW? Beet greens are a fantastic addition to green smoothies in place of, or in addition to, spinach. In fact, you can use young beet greens in place of spinach in many different recipes! Just make sure the greens are young, because large, mature leaves will be rough and bitter. Here is my favorite beet green smoothie recipe for you to try!

BEET GREENS AND SPINACH SMOOTHIE
YIELD—3 LARGE (16-OZ [473-ML]) SMOOTHIES

2-3 cups (241-362 g) ice

1 large banana (or 2 small), ripe

1 handful spinach

1 handful beet greens

3 tbsp (45 ml) orange juice concentrate

Water as needed

Combine all ingredients in a large blender, adding up to 1 cup (237 ml) or water to get all the blades moving. For a smoother smoothie, add more banana and to up the nutritional benefits, add more greens!

HOW TO MAKE NATURAL BEET DYE

Beet dye is incredibly simple to make and so beautiful to behold. Once your dye is complete, you can use it for plenty of fun crafts, such as dying yarn, creating frozen wreaths (see page 67) or creating pretty filter paper flowers (see page 68).

YIELD—3+ CUPS (708 ML)

5 to 6 medium-sized beets

Stainless steel medium-sized pot

3-4 cups (700–900 ml) of water

Slotted spoon

Cheesecloth

Jar for storage

1. Rinse any dirt off your beets, then peel.

2. Simmer the peels in the water at a low heat for 10 to 20 minutes.

3. Once your water is brilliantly red, pull beet peels out with a slotted spoon.

4. Allow the dye to cool, then pour through the cheesecloth into a jar.

5. Use the dye immediately or store in the refrigerator for up to a week.

DID YOU KNOW? A deep, dark ruby red is made from the flesh and peels of the beet root, but a lighter pink-red dye can be created from the beet stems. You might as well use up the whole beet, stems and all, and double up on your dye! You can dye natural fibers such as cotton and linen, yarn, paper or any other plant-based material you would like to experiment with!

Beet stems prepped for dye.

Beet stem dye is a lighter pink than beet root dye.

FROZEN ROSEMARY, CRANBERRY AND BEET JUICE CHRISTMAS WREATHS

These frozen wreaths are simple enough that a child can make them, but pretty enough for any décor! The trick is to make them in the dead of winter when temperatures stay consistently below freezing. You can add any beautiful bits you wish, but the real star is the beet juice. Yes, you read that correctly. I said beet juice. In fact, it is more beet stock than juice and simply uses up that beautiful natural dye from beet peelings. Go ahead and roast up the actual beets with ginger or use them in a delicious smoothie partnered with beet greens. All this project needs is the peels.

YIELD—2 TO 3 WREATHS

Peels from 5 to 6 beets

½ gallon (1 L) of water

Freezer-safe Bundt pan (ceramic or metal)

10 to 15 sprigs of rosemary or Christmas greens (optional)

2 to 3 cups (198 to 298 g) fresh or frozen cranberries (not dried)

Freezer, a flat freezing area

Parchment paper

Ribbon for hanging

1. Make beet juice by boiling the peels with the water.

2. Cool the beet juice to room temperature.

3. Strain any solid bits out of the juice with a slotted spoon.

4. Gently pour the juice into a round Bundt cake pan or circular mold. Be careful—it stains! Fill the pan almost to the top, leaving ½ inch (1.3 cm) or so to keep the juice from spilling when transferring the wreath into the freezer.

5. Add small cut pieces of rosemary (about 1 ½ inch [3.8 cm]) lightly on the surface of the juice. You can also push them into the juice, submerging them, but I prefer the way they look half in the juice and half out. Dot cranberries around the surface like tiny little ornaments. They will float!

6. Carefully transfer your pan into a flat surface in the freezer. Allow the wreath to fully freeze for 6 to 8 hours.

7. Once frozen, pull the wreath out of the freezer and allow the edges to melt slightly for 15 to 20 minutes. Once the edges are loose, gently turn the wreath out onto a large plate or bowl.

8. Use the ribbon to hang outdoors immediately in freezing temperatures, or put the wreath back into the freezer wrapped in parchment paper until ready to use.

Unmold frozen beet juice into a large bowl.

NOTE: Beet juice wreaths will stay frozen when the temperature is around or below 30°F (-1°C). If it gets warmer, the cranberries will fall out of the wreath and the birds will eat them. If the temperature gets above 40°F (4°C) or so, the entire wreath will melt. Make sure it will not bleed red onto an expensive surface, such as white marble.

BEET-DYED COFFEE FILTER PAPER FLOWERS

Coffee filter flowers are quite possibly the most inexpensive, yet beautiful craft that I have ever completed. The filters cost pennies and the beet juice and leftover coffee are basically free. They are easy to make while watching the children, watching TV or hanging out around a winter fire. Is there any time of the year when you need flowers *more* than when you are cuddled around a winter fire, trying to escape the harsh realities of ice and snow?

White (or brown) coffee filters (10 to 12 per flower)

Beet dye from boiled beet peels (page 64)

Leftover strong coffee

Stapler and staples

Felt and/or leather and hot glue to finish (optional)

Room spray or essential oil of your choice for scent (optional)

1. Fold and dip the coffee filters into the beet dye for various red and pink designs. Dip just barely on the edges and remove from the dye immediately for light lines around the edges of the petals. Try dipping the center of the filters, sides and edges for various effects.

2. Lay the filters out flat to dry on a surface that will not stain. My black granite counter top worked perfectly.

3. Once dry, dip in leftover strong coffee. Dip the entire filter or just portions to create different effects. Different levels of beet and coffee will produce varying degrees of pink, peach and crimson.

4. Allow the filters to dry flat again.

5. Once fully dry, stack 10 to 12 filters and fold the bunch in half. Staple in the middle.

6. Fold the opposite direction and staple again, on either side of your original staple.

7. Turn the filters right side up, so the staples are on the bottom. From the top down, grasp one filter at a time in your hand, scrunching to make "petals." Continue with all 10 to 12 layers.

8. Cinch the flower at the bottom and glue down the little "tail" that your stapled piece has created. Top with a circle of leather or felt to finish, if desired.

9. Optional: Spritz flowers with room spray or a couple dots of essential oil. They will hold scent for months!

Scent pretty beet-dyed flowers with long-lasting essential oils.

CHAPTER 7

FROM YOUR PANTRY—GINGER

With the industrialization of the food industry, the planting, growing and harvesting of vegetables has gained a sort of mystique around it. Buying a few tomato plants at the local big box store and planting a window box of strawberries might be the only experience one has with the process. That is quite sad, in my opinion. There are many plants that can't help but grow and the experience of watching a piece of food take root and grow is fascinating. If that plant happens to be a healing craft material, all the better! Join me as I showcase one of my favorite pantry plants: ginger.

GINGER FINGERS AND HOW TO MAKE THEM GROW

Ginger is technically a rhizome, and that knobby brown cluster grows under the earth while long, lean green stalks and leaves stretch toward the sun above. Ginger is used in a variety of teas, vegetable and meat dishes, and even cookies! Pickled ginger, candied ginger, powdered ginger or fresh—this rhizome can do it all!

To plant, first purchase a large piece of ginger from your supermarket or farmer's market. It should be quite inexpensive. Choose where you will house your potted ginger, considering its need for filtered light and temperate air. A south-facing windowsill will work perfectly!

Before peeling, cut 1- to 2-inch (2.5- to 5-cm) pieces of the "fingers" off of the ginger. Each piece must have nodes present, so do not cut the pieces too short or they will not sprout. The nodes are simply little bumps on the ginger where the roots will eventually sprout. A 1- to 2-inch (2.5- to 5-cm) piece from the ends of the ginger "fingers" is most likely to have at least one node.

Take your chunks of ginger and plant directly into a pot of potting soil, laying horizontally. The cut side should make contact with the soil, while the skin of the rhizome should remain slightly visible. Ginger is forgiving and might sprout from a few inches down in a pot, but prefers to be planted right at surface level. It is not alone, as ginger's cousin Iris also enjoys this soil placement.

Water the pot until water begins to seep out of the drainage hole in the bottom.

Leave the pot alone for at least a week and allow the soil to dry out a bit. Water once a week until you see little green sprouts emerging from the rhizome. At this point, you can water the plant when the soil is dry to the touch 1 inch (2.5 cm) under the surface. Yes, you simply use your finger to "feel" the soil. Do this once a week with all your plants and the ick factor is not so much a factor anymore. You are *growing* things! Also, remember to be patient. This process can take several months! If you do not see any green at all within 2 weeks, throw out your ginger chunks and try again with a slightly larger piece. I have a 70 to 80 percent success rate on ginger rhizomes. Sometimes there are just duds.

Once you have successfully grown a stalk with leaves, the race is on to flower. Remember to give ginger filtered light as it grows, considering its natural habitat under the canopy of tropical trees. You should see new growth pop up on the surface within 3 to 4 weeks. Once the plant has flowered, you can dig up the rhizome and surprise! Many more fingers will have formed! This same "trick" happens with most rhizomes, making them the perfect beginner experiment. Try Canna, asparagus or even turmeric if you want to branch out.

Remember how you removed the very end bits of ginger, leaving the "body" intact? That is the part you should peel and use for culinary purposes. We take those fingers off to plant for the following reasons:

> » They almost always have nodes on them poised to sprout.

> » They are awful to peel. Peeling the large middle section and chopping off the fingers to plant is much easier!

New ginger plants will grow from each little "finger" like these. One grocery store chunk of ginger can yield 5 to 6 plants or more!

THREE WAYS TO ROAST UP YOUR GINGER

Vegetables can be prepared in a multitude of ways, but in my humble opinion, there is no better way than to *roast* them. Low and slow, open to the fire, until they start to caramelize and "sugar up." That is the way to go in my book. Almost all root vegetables will taste delicious when roasted in this manner with a wee bit of ginger. Here are three ways to get your ginger fix:

» Use a chunk of ginger for a "scented" dish. If you do not like the strong taste of ginger, try this method for just a hint of its exotic charms. Peel a large chunk of ginger and roast it right along with your veggies, a bit of olive oil, salt and pepper. Halfway through roasting, give the dish a swirl and swoosh with the tongs, allowing the ginger to make its way around the dance floor a few times. Remove the ginger completely before serving.

» Try this same method with butternut squash or sweet potato, but instead of taking the ginger *out*, blend it *in*. Combined with a little butter and cream, a gingered mashup with these fall and winter favorites makes a delicious dish!

» If you are brave, dice that ginger up and roast it right alongside your chopped beets, mushrooms, potatoes, onions and garlic. Spicy, sweet and delicious!

HELP! MY GINGER WON'T GROW!

Sometimes plants just don't grow. Seeds are not viable, roots rot, diseases happen and conditions just aren't right. Some things you can fix and others are just the way nature works. If your ginger is not growing, here are a few things that might be the problem.

Have you watered enough? Without water, any plant will have a rough time getting started!

Have you watered too much?! The biggest hazard of indoor plants is typically the curse of caring too much. Plants indoors in winter do not need as much water as plants outdoors in the summer. Is the ginger you planted "squishy"? If so, it has rotted and it is time to start again.

Did you see a stalk start and then die off? If your ginger rhizome sprouted but then died, you might have been skimping on light. Try moving the pot to a warmer location with more sunlight.

Did you plant the rhizomes deeply in a pot of heavy soil and walk away? Remember, they need to be close to the surface! Try moving them closer to the surface of the pot, or start over with lighter potting soil.

DID YOU KNOW? Ginger can be frozen! Peel a few large pieces of ginger and place them in a plastic bag on your freezer door. Pull it out to shave or cut off chunks for cooking! It will last far longer than fresh ginger!

GINGER HIBISCUS BATH SALTS

This simple bath salt recipe is perfect for when you are feeling a bit under the weather. The ginger is beneficial to both hair and skin, providing increased blood flow, astringent properties and even anti-aging benefits! I enjoy ginger when I am sick because just the scent seems to quell nausea a bit. The Epsom salt in the mix has a litany of benefits for the skin and body. Epsom salt is not actually salt. Rather, it is a naturally occurring pure mineral compound of magnesium and sulfate. That magnesium seeps into the skin during a long bath, easing stress, relaxing muscles and reducing inflammation. The hibiscus flowers offer a pretty color to the bath and also smell quite nice with a subtle floral scent.

Before assembling your bath salts, you will need to grow, dry and grind ginger. Of course, you can just pop in to the local grocery store for some culinary-grade ground ginger as well! If you are starting with ginger root, simply peel and slice the fresh ginger and allow it to dry until crispy in a dehydrator or oven set on 200°F (193°C). (Skip ahead to the citrus chapter [page 130] and you can double-time it while drying grapefruit and orange! Ginger goes well with both.)

Once it is completely dry and crisp, grind ginger with a mortar and pestle, food processor or even a clean peppercorn grinder.

YIELD—6 TO 7 BATHS

1 cup (150 g) ground ginger (DIY or find at any grocery store)

2 cups (273 g) Epsom salt (available in bulk from club stores, also in grocery stores)

½ cup (about 100 g) dry hibiscus flowers or rose petals (found in bulk on Amazon)

1. Simply combine your ingredients in whatever jar suits your fancy. You can make large or small batches; just keep the ratios the same. I leave my salt mix in pretty layers, displayed in the bathroom until I need it.

2. Give the jar a little shake before decanting ½ cup (85 g) into a warm bath to enjoy!

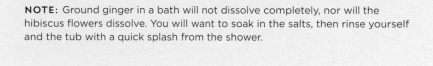

NOTE: Ground ginger in a bath will not dissolve completely, nor will the hibiscus flowers dissolve. You will want to soak in the salts, then rinse yourself and the tub with a quick splash from the shower.

Make "in-a-jar" gifts in layers for a pretty effect, but make sure to shake before using!

FRAGRANT AND FRESH GINGER SOAP BARS

I call these little bars "caterpillar bars" because they are made in a baking mold that has an elongated, curved shape (like Twinkies!) These particular bars use fresh ginger along with various essential oils and other add-ins. You can experiment with any "sharp" scent, as almost anything in the citrus or mint family will complement ginger well. I love to play with combinations of tangerine, lemongrass, green tea powder and chia seed for a variety of scents and textures. Give these fragrant and pretty bars as gifts or hoard them all for yourself!

8 CATERPILLAR BARS

½ lb (227 g) shea butter melt-and-pour soap (available online or at craft stores)

Microwave-safe bowl, double boiler or small crafting crockpot

4 medium ginger roots, peeled

"Caterpillar" baking mold or silicone/non-stick mold of your choice

Various add-ins, such as citrus essential oils, powdered spices or tiny seeds

Toothpicks

1. Melt the soap in a microwave, double boiler or small crafting crockpot. Slowly melt the soap in 3- to 4-inch (7.5- to 10-cm) chunks. Do not boil!

2. While the soap is melting, grate the peeled ginger into the bottoms of your molds.

3. Pour the melted soap over the top of the ginger and add in 6 to 7 drops of essential oil per bar. I used tangerine and lemongrass, which were both pretty awesome.

4. Stir in add-ins with a toothpick. For a few bars, I omitted the citrus scents and added green tea powder and chia seed instead. Feel free to have fun with various mixes!

5. These soaps look cute packed together, flat sides in if using the caterpillar-shaped mold, and twisted in twine.

NOTE: Unless you specifically purchase a soap that "suspends" ingredients, some settling will occur on the curved side of the soap. In these particular soaps, I find the ginger and green tea settling to be quite beautiful. If you would like the mixture to be evenly mixed throughout, purchase a soap labeled for suspension.

CHAPTER 8

FROM YOUR PANTRY—POTATOES

Potatoes might seem too pedestrian. They might seem dirty, coarse and common. Those things are all true. Potatoes are perhaps the humblest of crops, yet they provide nutrition, an easy growing habit and make a surprisingly fun craft material! You don't even need to run to the nursery to start growing potatoes; you probably just need to look in your pantry!

HOW TO GROW PANTRY POTATOES

Have you ever peeked into the pantry and noticed weird little growths on the potatoes? Did you throw them out? *For shame*! Those little weird green things were potatoes wanting to *grow* and you could have had a nice new crop of potatoes! You can start potato plants indoors in late spring to go outdoors in summer or grow directly in the garden from late spring to late summer.

All you need to get started is new potting soil or very nice, loamy garden soil, potatoes and a knife. It's important that you use new potting soil or loamy garden soil. While potatoes are very easy to grow, the one thing they really need is soft soil that they can grow into. Picture a potato trying to grow underground in hard soil. It just doesn't work!

All potatoes have little "eyes" on them—little dimples or knobs where the skin is not smooth. Those are the source of new life and new potatoes. If they are already starting to grow, you have a head start. Simply cut off the corner of the potato with around 1- to 2-inches (2.5- to 5-cm) of potato flesh. Each chunk should have several "eyes." Allow the potato chunks to sit overnight in the open air to form a slight skin on the potato flesh.

Then simply plant the chunks flesh side down, "weird little growth" pointing up towards the sun and make sure they are 1 to 2 inches (2.5 to 5 cm) below the surface of the soil. Water the pot or plot until the soil of the top is moist or water emerges from the drainage hole in the bottom of the pot. Do not water again for 4 to 5 days or until the first 2 inches (5 cm) of soil are dry. You want the potato to have moisture, but not be soaking wet. Water again when the top 2 inches (5 cm) of soil dry out and continue in this manner until sprouts appear.

In 2 to 3 weeks, you will see stems emerging from the soil. Go ahead and give the plants more water at this point, then hold off watering again until the top 2 inches (5 cm) of soil are dry. This is the point where your plant will really need some strong light. Place it outdoors or in a greenhouse. Potato plants with insufficient light will grow tall and weak seeking the light, eventually toppling over and breaking the stem. When given strong sunlight, the potato will grow into a strong, grounded plant and then flower. After flowering, stop watering the plant. The flower stalk and leaves will turn brown and might fall over. This is your cue to go digging for potatoes! You can use a shovel or trowel, but you run the risk of piercing and ruining potatoes. You see, while that plant was growing vertically *up* towards the sun, the plant was growing in all different directions *under* the soil, creating potatoes in the most unlikely of spots. It is much more fun to harvest potatoes with your hands and it is akin to a treasure hunt for kids, so put them to work! Potatoes are ready to eat or use for crafts fresh from the ground or can be stored for use weeks later. Store potatoes "dirty" (no rinsing!) for a longer shelf life.

GROW FANCY FINGERLING POTATOES FROM TRIMMINGS

Fingerling potatoes are adorable little potatoes that appropriately look like knobby little fingers. They come in various colors, with purple being the most beautiful, and the yellows tasting the best. The problem? They cost double or triple the cost of traditional round potatoes at the grocery store. While they are convenient for fast cooking and certainly look cute on a plate, I do not know if they are cute enough for a triple-it-up price hike. Do you? It is a good thing then that fingerling potatoes can be grown just as easily as regulars in your own kitchen garden.

PLANTING FINGERLINGS

You can buy potato "sets" ready for planting in spring, but I like to simply buy a variety pack of fingerlings from Costco and chop them up for planting. The technique is the same as with regular potatoes (see previous section), but you will plant fingerlings slightly closer to the surface of the soil and they will often grow faster than the large potatoes. Harvest when the potato plant dries up and falls over, then enjoy them on the plate or in a craft!

POTATO CRAFTS FOR PENNIES

Potatoes are so easy to grow and so inexpensive to buy that they are the perfect choice for home crafting materials. From stamps to dyes, these humble materials are fantastic tools for your grown and gathered craft arsenal. Gather up the kids and some home harvested potatoes and get ready to make some fun stamps, carvings and maybe even dinner!

POTATO CRAFTS FOR PENNIES (CONTINUED)

SUPPLIES

Metal cookie cutter. Plastic cookie cutters are usually not strong enough, so stick with metal!

Clay carving kit. These are inexpensive tools that come in a kit made to carve designs into clay. They work fantastically on potatoes!

Printing surfaces. These surfaces could be a T-shirt, hand towel, paper, cardboard, eggs, muslin or anything else you choose!

CARVING POTATO STAMPS

You can carve just about anything out of a potato and use it as a stamp, but my favorite method is to use the humble metal cookie cutter. A cookie cutter is strong enough to cut into the potato flesh and provides a nice clean line. Anything from Easter eggs to Halloween bats to Christmas bells can be created with the marriage of a potato and cookie cutter! Simply press the metal halfway down into the potato flesh. If you push the cutter all the way into the potato, it can be difficult to remove. Pull the cookie cutter out, then carve the outside portions away, creating a sculpture in relief. A fun design is to use a large potato and two heart shapes, curved sides in. The result is a set of charming little wings!

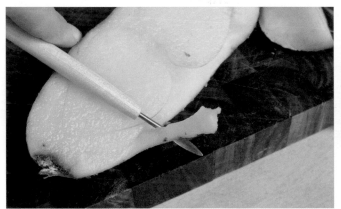
Carve flesh from edges of potatoes.

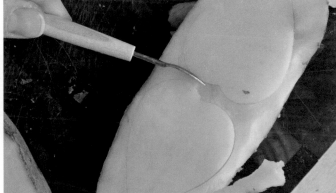
Use a curved carver to carefully carve details.

Remove any remaining potato flesh.

Use stamps to create wings or hearts!

STAMPING PROCESS

Once you have created your stamp, you can go two directions: paint or dye. (*Sounds* like a great T-shirt, doesn't it?) Craft paints and fabric paints are fairly inexpensive and work well with potatoes, but you might also experiment with natural dyes, bleach or commercial fabric dye. Dip the stamp carefully into the paint or dye, allowing the potato flesh to soak up a little of the liquid for a strong impression. Allow the stamp to drip if necessary, then slowly move the potato stamp to your fabric or painting surface and place it down once firmly. Hold for 1 to 2 seconds. Release straight up to avoid smearing the stamp. It is also helpful to spear your potato chunks with a carving tool to use as a "handle" if the pieces are small (see photos below).

PRIMED STAMPS

Alternatively, if you would like your stamps to be a bit less crisp and clear, you will need to "prime" them before stamping. By prime, I simply mean prepare. You still need to get a good coating of paint or dye onto and into the potato, but then stamp off the crispness and goopiness on a scrap piece of cardboard. Once the stamp starts fading a bit, apply to your surface for a weathered look.

SLIDING STAMPS

While playing around with different textures, I found that an organic design from a shaved potato stamp (see photo below) can make really cool textures when you slide it across your canvas. Simply shave a bark-like design into a long and tall potato and give it a light coating of paint. Place the potato at the top or edge of your canvas, paper or fabric and gently drag the potato to the opposite edge. The result is completely unique patterns that vary slightly on each application and from stamp to stamp. Potato stamps will last up to 24 hours, but begin to dry up and curl after a day. Dispose of the potatoes in the trash, rather than compost due to the paint and/or bleach.

Use a carving tool as the "handle" of your stamp.

Curl pieces of potato flesh away to create a texture stamp.

FROM YOUR PANTRY—POTATOES —

POTATO CANDY

When I was trying to come up with fun activities to do with potatoes, my husband suggested potato candy. At first, I thought he was crazy and the idea sounded quite awful. However, once he started describing his grandmother's process of potato candy making, it started to make a little more sense. Just imagine replacing the butter in mashed potatoes with confectioner's sugar and you have an idea of the basic premise of potato candy. In fact, the potato is more of a binder and the flavor is of straight delicious sugar. Add in peanut butter and a simple rolling technique and you end up with fun, delicious little slices!

YIELD—15 TO 20 PIECES

2 medium-sized potatoes, peeled and cut into chunks

1 to 2 cups (236 to 473 ml) of boiling water

1 tsp salt

1 tsp milk

2 tsp (10 g) butter

2 lb (900 g) bag of confectioner's sugar (powdered sugar)

At least 4 cups (950 g) peanut butter (smooth, chunky, natural or honey)

The order of instructions and additions in this recipe is very important. Follow each step precisely, particularly in regards to cooling or chilling ingredients.

1. Start by making mashed potatoes. Place chunks of peeled potatoes into boiling water until they are just covered. Boil 10 to 12 minutes or until they are soft and easy to pierce with a fork. Drain off water and mash potatoes with the salt, milk and butter. The mashed potatoes should be very thick, but not lumpy. Think thick German mashed potatoes, not super smooth, liquid-like potatoes. Place in the refrigerator to chill for at least 1 hour.

2. Take *very cold* potatoes and mix with 2 cups (250 g) of powdered sugar. If you use regular sugar, brown sugar or warm/hot potatoes, the recipe will fail. Continue to add powdered sugar until the mixture turns into a foldable dough. You will use up to 2 pounds (900 g) of sugar.

3. Sprinkle a baking sheet with powdered sugar and spread out the dough as thin as possible with your fingers, about ¼- to ½-inch (6- to 13-mm) thick. Chill in the refrigerator for 10 to 12 minutes.

4. This step requires 4 cups (950 g) of peanut butter in the variety you choose. Honey peanut butter makes a sweet addition, chunky adds some crunch and natural or smooth peanut butter is a more subtle complement to the potato dough. Whichever peanut butter you choose, make certain that it is warm, "loose" and well mixed. *Do not* melt in the microwave. Rather, leave the peanut butter out at room temperature or warming in the sun until it is very easy to mix with a spoon.

5. Add dollops of warm peanut butter to the top of the chilled dough and carefully spread into a thin layer. The dough should be workable at this point.

6. Roll dough into a log, moving slowly and carefully. Use a spatula or your fingers to pull dough up and into a log, much like a jelly roll. Squeeze enough to make the layers touch, but be careful not to squeeze so hard that the layers actually mix and/or squeeze out of the log. Chill in refrigerator for 30 minutes.

7. Slice the log into ½-inch (1.3-cm) slices with a sharp knife, wiping the knife clean with a paper towel between each cut. Keep chilled and covered until serving.

VARIATIONS

Try rolling the edges in shaved chocolate or nuts for a fun twist!

As another variation, turn the traditional candies into delicious coconut snowballs! Follow steps 1 to 5, then coat your hands in powdered sugar and roll the sliced pinwheels into balls. Coat the balls in shaved coconut. Chill and serve.

NOTE: This recipe comes from a tradition of German grandmothers who took leftover mashed potatoes from Sunday dinner and made them into something magical. You can certainly use your leftovers as well or start the recipe from scratch with step 2.

82   CRAFTING WITH NATURE

CHAPTER 9

FROM YOUR PANTRY— ONIONS TO EAT & DYE

The classic onion is a nice bright white and is used in hundreds of dishes to grand effect. A world without onions would be a flavorless world indeed! However, the world of onions is not limited to the common white. In fact, there are plenty of alliums beyond those that you will find in the grocery bins. Onions are part of the allium family and there are plenty of ornamental alliums along with our culinary types. Both the edibles and the ornamentals are easy to grow, cheap to produce and easy to store for crafting.

FOUR TYPES OF ONIONS AND WHY YOU WANT TO GROW THEM ALL

RED ONIONS (PURPLE!) - SETS

My favorite onion of all is perhaps the red onion, in part due to its inaccurate name. Is there any question that the red onion is in fact purple? Are we too far gone to change the name? Bad name or no, the red onion has the exact level of bite to use raw and thinly sliced on a variety of sandwiches and salads, but can also fry up nicely or substitute for whites in a pinch. Red onions are commonly found as "sets" to grow in the garden and are quite inexpensive.

VIDALIA AND OTHER SWEETS - PANTRY/GROCERY

Deliciously sweet and luscious, Maui, Vidalia and Walla Walla are the dessert element of the onion family. All have a high sugar content, making these onions the type that you can eat simply roasted and buttered—*yum*! These sweet onions are a bit harder to find in the garden center, but more easily found in the vegetable aisles. Grow these sweets by using cut tops, sliced cleanly and planted cut side down into soft soil.

SHALLOTS, PEARLS AND CIPPOLINIS - PANTRY/GROCERY OR SETS

These are the specialty onions and your best bet for return on investment (of time and money) in the home garden. Shallots are used for delicate dishes, particularly French cuisine. Pearl onions are small little onions and show up on Grandma's table mixed with green beans or peas. Cippolinis are my favorite of the bunch, with a slightly sweet flavor and adorable flattened shape. All three can be grown in the home garden, but I skip the pearls as they are too small and laborious to be worth harvesting.

CHIVES, SPRING ONIONS AND OTHER "GREENS" - PLANTS, NOT SEEDS

One of the first plants you should try growing is the basic chive. The best bet for beginners is to buy a small plant, rather than attempting to grow them by seed. They are hard to kill and delicious when cut young and fresh. Try them on a classic summer potato salad or cold potato soup (previous page) and then get back to me. You will be changed!

Chives are also quite expensive to buy at the grocery store, but easy to keep year after year in a corner of your garden. Note that they are *so* tough that they can take over your garden, so consider planting a pot instead of planting directly in a vegetable garden. Alternatively, if you really like chives, plant a small bed of them all to themselves. You will never be without! A second benefit of chives is the adorable little purple blooms that come later in the season. Note that the chive blossoms *are* edible and provide a bit of color to salads, but I do not particularly like them. Once chives have flowered, the green leaf will be too old to taste good, so you have a few options. Just let them grow and move onto the tomatoes in the garden *or* cut them back to 1 inch (1.3 cm) from the ground and new, fresh chives will grow. Those new chives will be delicious and perfect for consuming!

All onions grow "greens" on top of the soil, but some taste much better than others. A rule of thumb is that the larger the onion that grows below the soil, the less desirable the greens. Spring onions and the greens from shallots are quite nice, but chives are my hands down favorite. Another added benefit? Both chives and green onions will survive and thrive even with a bit of snow! They are one of the first peeks of green you will see each spring and one of the last plants to bite the dust in fall.

GIFTING ONIONS

Onions are one of the easiest crops to grow in a home garden and they can make a wonderful gift! Try gifting a batch of cream soup topped with chives or your famous red potato salad complete with cippolinis and red onions! Why not make a flower arrangement with those beautiful purple chive blossoms? Wouldn't your neighbor appreciate some pickled onions, cauliflower and carrots to top her summer salads? Perhaps the best gift of all is a 3-foot-tall (90-cm) onion gifted from your 6-year-old to his grandpa. A gardening grandpa couldn't be prouder!

ONION DYES AND OTHER NATURAL COLORINGS

The humble onion actually makes an excellent crafting material. Collect the peels and skins from onions to create beautiful, free crafting dyes. Onion-dyed Easter eggs have been seen many times and over again, but the same method can be applied to any natural, porous surface. The process is simple and basically requires boiling onion skins in water to a desired strength and then applying the dye to natural materials. Here are a few tips.

» Onion skin dying is unique in that it does not need a mordant. Mordant is a chemical that helps the dye adhere to and stay on natural dyed products. If you choose to use a mordant with onion skin dye, the color will intensify and darken, but it is not necessary to the craft.

» A simple mordant can be used by mixing cream of tartar and alum. I buy these in bulk at a discount grocery store where the prices are super cheap and the quantities are large! You will want a ratio of two parts alum to one part cream of tartar. An 8-quart-crock (7570 g) batch of skins will require 1 teaspoon alum to ½ teaspoon cream of tartar.

» The color of your natural dye will change depending on whether you use a mordant or not. You can choose to use a mordant to lighten and brighten the color of your onion skin dyed products, but it is not necessary.

» There are natural mordants that you can find in your pantry including salt, vinegar, fermenting fruit and of course, stale urine. I stay away from that one personally, but if you are ever in a pinch, it works.

» The colors of natural dyes might surprise you! While some, like blueberry, turn out as you might expect, others create wildly different colors than you might imagine. Red onion skins, for example, turn out a green dye, while green tea turns out a yellow dye. Red cabbage turns out a blue dye and beet tops turn out a muted green. You never know what to expect and experimenting with natural dyes and the changes you can effect via mordants is fun!

» One of my favorite onion dyes is the yellow onion, which turns out a beautiful, deep crimson. To get the most intense color, put the skins of 5 to 6 yellow onions and 2 teaspoons (10 ml) white vinegar into a large pot. Add as little water as you can until the skins are covered when weighted down with a smaller pot. Boil the mixture 5 minutes or so until the water is a strong, deep red. This dye can be used to boil eggs for Easter, dye linens that have become coffee stained or for any other creative project you can come up with!

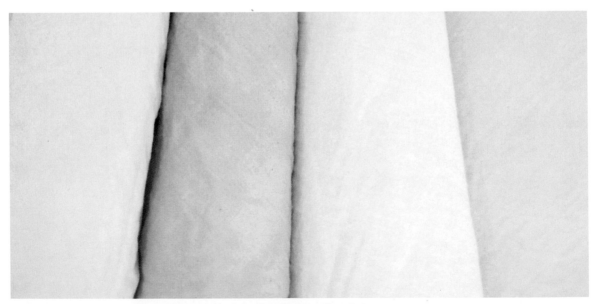

Various shades of earth tones can be made by using various onion skin dyes and mordants.

QUICK ONION-DYED MUSLIN BAGS

Muslin bags are a great way to dress up little gifts that might seem insubstantial on their own. For instance, a handful of your favorite tree peony seeds, a vial of handmade coconut oil or a handful of lavender plucked fresh from your garden all make delightful gifts, but need to be contained. A plastic baggy will do, of course, but we can do better!

These little muslin bags are very cheap online in bulk, but the ones I got are a whitish muslin with yellow and red embroidery on two different lines. The colors really clash for me, so I decided to give them an onion dye bath.

Medium-sized stainless steel pot (*not* aluminum or copper, as these can affect the outcome)

3–4 cups (700–900 ml) of water

Peels and outer skins from 5 to 6 large yellow and red onions (save inner flesh for cooking)

2 tbsp (30 ml) white vinegar

Muslin bags (DIY from lengths of bulk muslin and embroidery thread or buy in bulk inexpensively)

1. Fill the pot with 3 to 4 cups (700 to 900 ml) of water and turn to high. Cover with a lid to bring to a boil faster.

2. When the water reaches a rolling boil, put the onion skins into the water. Use an equal combination of yellow and red onions for a nice deep reddish-tan or experiment with different onion peels and skin types to create your own color combination.

3. Reduce heat to low-medium until the skins are bubbling, but not boiling.

4. Add the white vinegar.

5. Allow the mixture to simmer on low for 10 to 15 minutes while the color extracts fully.

6. Turn off heat and allow the mixture to cool slightly. Remove onions and add them to the compost or trash.

7. Place muslin bags in warm dye and stir with a wooden spoon to saturate. Make sure the bags do not have creases where the dye cannot penetrate.

8. Allow the bags to soak for 4 to 5 hours, stirring once an hour or so.

9. Remove from dye, *do not squeeze* and lay out on a drying surface. Allow bags to sit for 1 to 2 days, drying and fully soaking up dye.

10. Your bags are now fully dried, but will smell like onions! Give them a gentle soap and water bath that will remove the smell, but leave the dye. Color will lighten slightly.

11. Allow bags to dry fully, iron if desired and start gifting all your little natural gifts to friends and family!

From left to right: Muslin bags dyed with a double concentrated onion dye, the recipe above, after washing and without dye.

section four

GROWING THE BACKYARD GARDEN MAINSTAYS

Lavender and lamb's ear. Rose and citrus. The almighty summer tomato! If you have gardened for a while or inherited a small backyard garden, chances are you have grown at least a few of these plants. Tomatoes are typically the first plant young gardeners try when they experiment with edibles, while garden favorites like lavender and lamb's ear often show up in the humblest of gardens. When a gardener gets serious, roses and citrus start to show up in droves. They are two of the most difficult, yet most rewarding plants to grow.

The crafting supplies in this chapter are plentiful and luxurious. From floral scents that can make a grown man stop and take pause to soft little lamb's ears that make babies sit and pick for hours at a time, these plants are favorites for a reason! Join me as I show you how to craft wreaths, soaps, lotion bars and bows from the leaves, stems and flowers of these fabulous plants!

CHAPTER 10
THE MOST CLASSIC
HERB IN CRAFTING—LAVENDER

Lavender is the fragrance that can sing above almost any other, and stand out amidst the more subtle players in the garden. That scent has endurance too! While many perennial flowers fragrance the garden for a fortnight, lavender will keep producing almost all summer. Once the flowers are stripped from the stems, that scent keeps going for years to come. That simple endurance makes lavender a joy to work with and a perfect candidate for wreaths and the most amazing smelling perfume.

HOW TO GROW LAVENDER FROM SEED AND KEEP IT ALIVE!

Lavender is not an easy plant to grow from seed, but it can be done. If you are a beginner gardener, you should start by buying a small lavender *plant* and once successful, try your hand at starting from seed.

GROWING LAVENDER SEED BASICS

First and foremost, start with a lavender variety known to grow well from seed. Burpee offers several that do well and provide consistently identical plants including Lavender Lady, Traditional Provence and Lacy Frill, a white lavender. If you buy cheap lavender seed, you will end up with a bunch of different-looking lavender once they actually put on leaves and then bloom. While this is not a huge problem, it can be frustrating if you want one specific look for a hedge.

Once you have chosen your seed, you want to choose a growing medium. Regular old garden soil is *not* a good choice for lavender. Native to Mediterranean climates, lavender likes sandy soils that drain very quickly. It does not like to have drought conditions, however. In short, you are going to dance a water waltz with your lavender plants and either too much or too little will be death for the plants. For those who enjoy a little challenge, carry on. Get a nice sandy, quick draining potting soil from your local garden center and fill small peat pots almost to the top. If you do not want to spend the money on peat pots, you can absolutely make your own biodegradable pots. Folded newspaper or toilet paper rolls make perfect little pots. You want a pot that can be planted directly in the ground so that the lavender seedlings have the best chance of surviving the transplant

Water the soil *before* planting the seeds. Watering seeds can be difficult business, especially when you are giving them their first shower. By watering the soil first, you will reduce the chance of a flood sending your seeds onto the floor and into oblivion.

Once water runs out of the drainage holes of your pots, plant 2-3 seeds in each small peat pot. Lavender seeds need light to germinate and are tiny, so simply let them fall onto the potting soil and press them gently to make contact with the soil. They do not need to be, nor should they be, buried.

Place the seedlings in a south-facing window and offer them some warmth from a heat mat if possible. Your rate of germination will most likely increase and will definitely speed up with the addition of heat. Water when the top two inches (5 cm) of soil is dry. Remember that it is easier to *over* water lavender than to under water it.

Once your little plants start to grow, make certain to rotate them every once in a while so that they don't lean towards the light and create leggy seedlings.

When your lavenders are 4 to 5 inches (10 to 13 cm) tall with several sets of leaves, you can plant your biodegradable pots directly into the ground. Again, keep plants watered, but make sure the soil drains quickly. The two main causes of death for lavender is a lack of rainfall *or* standing water at its roots that does not drain well. It is a dance, y'all.

NOTE: If you are transplanting small plants that you purchased, the basics of care are the same. Make sure the plant has full sun, give it well-draining soil and water it in well to get it established.

CREATE LAVENDER WREATHS IN SEVERAL STUNNING SHAPES

Lavender is a perfect natural crafting material because it dries beautifully. Lavender also keeps its perfume much longer than other dried flowers. If you harvest and bend the flowers while still fresh, they can be manipulated into a variety of shapes. Join me as I show you three of my favorite shapes!

LAVENDER CIRCLE WREATH

Creating a circular wreath is done by bunching lavender and attaching it to a wire frame. Simply cut lavender stalks when the flowers first begin to open on a cool summer morning. All herbs are at their best when cut early in the day when the essential oils are most concentrated. Make sure to cut bundles of 15 to 20 stems at a time, all the same length. Tie your bundles into bunches by the stems as you harvest each handful. Once you have 8 to 10 bunches, attach the bundles to a medium-sized wire wreath frame with clear fishing line, making sure the flowers "fan" out towards the outer rim of the wreath. Flowers will dry in place and the wreath will last for several seasons, if not several years.

SKINNY LAVENDER HEART WREATH

There are many variations of the heart wreath, but I prefer them to either be very skinny or very, very fat. Somewhere in between just seems a little underdone or too busy. To make a skinny little heart wreath, a cheap wire hanger is your best friend. Simply bend it into a heart shape, then hot glue small bunches of lavender along the frame. Alternatively, pre-shaped wire frames are available for purchase.

FAT LAVENDER HEART WREATH

A fully covered lavender heart is a nice change of pace. For this design, you will need a styrofoam heart base, toothpick and shorts pieces of lavender. This can be a great project for little stems that get broken while making larger wreaths! Simply stick stems into the Styrofoam, using a toothpick as a guide. Start in the middle and work your way out to the edges until the heart is full and lush!

MINI LAVENDER HEART

When crafting with lavender, you will most likely have an abundance of loose flowers that have fallen off. Use them by gluing them onto a cardboard heart form. Add a leather strip or grosgrain ribbon to hang from a doorknob.

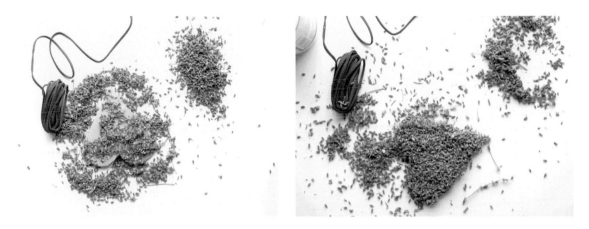

LAVENDER STAR

This lavender star is super simple and darling over a doorknob, hung on a mailbox post or as a gift topper any time of year! Start with a grapevine star frame (see page 33) and place 2- to 3-inch (5- to 7.5-cm) lavender stems into the frame, making sure the flowers are visible. Continue "stuffing" until the star is full to bursting! This is another great project for leftover little bits of lavender.

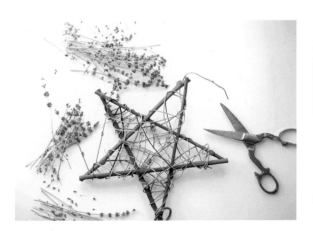
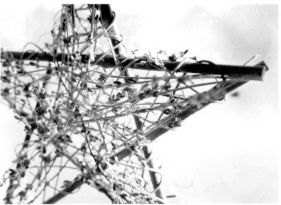

DIY LAVENDER SOLID PERFUME EGGS

I tend to use lavender oil instead of fresh flower buds when making most toiletries because the scent doesn't cross over into a "cooked" lavender scent. Using commercially pressed essential oils also adds a powerful lavender smell with just a few drops, making it perfect for these small perfume eggs.

I had honestly never heard of solid perfume until I stumbled upon a little tub of it one afternoon while shopping at Anthropologie. Wow! So much scent in such a little package! I loved the idea of a tiny little package of perfume, ready to use anywhere without lugging around a heavy glass bottle. When I stumbled upon some vintage metal Easter eggs, I knew they would make perfect molds. Garnished with fresh lavender straight from the backyard, these eggs make the perfect little gift!

YIELD—3 EGGS OR SMALL CONTAINERS

2 tbsp (30 g) yellow beeswax pellets

Microwave-safe bowl or crafting crockpot

1 tsp olive oil

Lavender essential oil, plus your choice of tangerine, bergamot or lemongrass essential oil

Cute metal or glass quarter ounce containers

Dried lavender flowers (optional)

1. Add the beeswax pellets to a small crafting crockpot or microwave-safe bowl in the microwave. Heat until the beeswax melts down, but *do not boil*. In the microwave, go 30 seconds at a time and let the glass cool slightly in between heatings.

2. Once the wax is fully liquid, add the olive oil, 30 drops of lavender essential oil and 15 drops of additional complimentary oils. This may seem like a lot of fragrance oil, but remember, this is a perfume. The scents are concentrated and a small dab behind the ears is all you need. Combine lavender with your choice of tangerine, bergamot or lemongrass for your choice of scent.

3. Once the oils are added, carefully stir them to incorporate and heat once again if needed to make a fully liquid mixture.

4. Decant the mixture into your choice of small container. If you would like to add dried lavender or any other dry herb to the mix, place the dry bits in the container first and then pour wax mixture over the top. Solids will settle to the bottom.

5. Allow the perfumes to dry fully and then use as a travel perfume or simply unmold them from the containers. The unmolded perfumes can be rubbed directly onto wrists or neck while the travel pots are used by rubbing a finger onto the perfume, then onto the skin.

DID YOU KNOW? You can make lip balm and solid perfume with the very same ingredients! Perfume requires much more scent (from the essential oils) and more beeswax to keep the mixture very solid, and it releases only a bit per use. Lip balm requires more olive oil and much less scent so that it rubs onto skin easily to moisturize!

CHAPTER 11

RUGOSAS, ROSEBUDS, ROSEHIPS & ROSE CRAFTS

The scent of rose is as common as coffee, yet royal as myrrh. While readily available in nurseries, roses can be fairly difficult to grow. Though fussy, roses are still a widely popular flower and fragrance. In this chapter, we dive into both growing and crafting with rose scent and potions, offering solutions for gardeners, crafters and those who love both!

THE ROSE FOR BEGINNERS

While traditional roses have their beauty and grace, the roses I love include the wild and rugged rugosa rose and English David Austin roses. The David Austin roses are bred from "old" roses that are tougher than classic hybrids, and bred to retain the classic rose scents. They are expensive and luxurious and when one blooms, I use them in arrangements. I don't have enough David Austin's to use them for crafting, so for crafting with rosebuds, petals and hips, I turn to the good old rugosas.

If you think you cannot grow roses, you haven't tried a rugosa yet. They are tough as nails and have the thorns to prove it. They will put out new canes every growing season, creating new plants for you without any interference and they will grow the most delightful, large and juicy hips that you have ever seen. Hips are the fruit of the rose and almost nonexistent on classic tea roses. If you are trying to invite bees into the garden, you can plant no better plant than a rugosa for the bees literally *roll* around in the flowers each summer.

If you want to grow a rugosa, you might check out your neighbor's garden or wild, overgrown and empty lots. Cuttings taken from a bush where you can observe its color and growth habit is the best way to secure a beautiful hedge of rugosa roses. Here is how it is done.

1. Select a rugosa with a flower color you enjoy and a round, bushy growth pattern, as opposed to straggly stems.

2. Select rose canes that are green and fresh, yet mature enough to be larger than a pencil in circumference.

3. Take 6-inch (15-cm) cuttings with a sharp, clean knife or pruners.

4. Dip cuttings in rooting hormone for added success, or simply sink the cuttings 2 inch (5 cm) deep into rich potting soil.

5. While all cuttings might not "take," my success rate with roses is always around 50 to 60 percent. Plan to take multiple cuttings to ensure you are able to propagate as many plants as you want.

RUGOSA ROSE PRUNING

Rugosas are wild and rugged; thus they don't need much care to survive. However, to ensure a pretty, rounded bush, many blooms and large hips, you must prune. Rugosas are best pruned in the spring, and some gardeners cut them down all the way to the ground, leaving just a few inches of stem from each cane. I tend to prune a bit more lightly because the rugosas form structure in my garden design. Always prune out anything brown first. Both completely dead wood and old canes will be a shade of brown and neither will produce well.

While pruning, be aware that rugosas are very thorny. Use leather gloves to handle the canes, and consider using tongs to hold down cane ends while you cut the base so that the cane does not fling up to hit you in the face or fall onto your toes! Using the canes as bonfire fuel is the best way to dispose of the prunings.

White rugosa rose in bloom.

Common magenta rugosa roses are bee magnets.

SIMPLE ROSEWATER

Rosewater has been around for centuries and has many uses, from culinary to cosmetic to religious. There are factories, large and small, devoted to the distillation of rose into a crystal clear water, but for our purposes, we are going to stick with a simple DIY. This rosewater can be used in culinary and cosmetic applications, such as for the Rosewater Face Toner (page 101). Keep in mind that it has no preservatives, so make sure it is stored in the refrigerator. Also make certain that the rose petals you use are chemical-free and "culinary grade." You can buy culinary grade rose petals, but the best option is to grow your own rose petals without chemicals and harvest them yourself!

If you gather rose petals from your backyard, you want to get the moisture out of them before using them in projects so that the oils are concentrated as much as possible. A dehydrator works, but they will also dry just fine lying out on towels on the kitchen table. They may stain, however, so use old linens!

YIELD—1 TO 2 CUPS (200 TO 500 ML)

8 cups (1.9 L) distilled water (available at the grocery store)

Large stockpot

1 cup (12 g) culinary grade dried rose petals

Colander and a small mesh screen

1. Place the distilled water into the stockpot. Filtered water that you are able to drink from the tap can be utilized, but distilled water will make purer rosewater that lasts longer without preservatives.

2. Add the dried rose petals.

3. Turn the heat to high to get it going, but cover and reduce to low immediately when bubbles begin to form. You want to extract the oils, but not boil the petals.

4. After 20 to 30 minutes of barely simmering, turn the heat off, but do *not* remove the lid. Allow the steam to settle back into the rosewater.

5. Strain the rose "pulp" from the rosewater. I strained once in a colander and once through a small mesh screen to remove all bits of rose. (You can use this pulp for rose beads. See page 106.) Allow the rosewater to cool.

6. Store cooled rosewater in the refrigerator in a sealed container.

HEALING ROSE INFUSION AND SALVE

For as many projects as there are for rosewater, you can add up just as many for rose oil. The process is just as simple too! Once your infused rose oil has had the chance to soak for 2 to 3 days, you can use it for many crafts and DIYs. One of my favorites is a pretty healing salve. This recipe uses basic materials, whips up quickly and smells amazing! You will love the way this salve softens and heals dry skin and you will be addicted to the amazing, pure and natural rose fragrance.

YIELD—3 TO 4 SMALL JARS

INFUSION

Dried culinary grade and chemical-free rose petals and/or buds

Culinary grade oil (olive, walnut or almond oils work well)

Jar with sealed lid for storage

SALVE

¼ cup (59 ml) coconut oil

1 cup (236 ml) petroleum jelly (generic or name brand)

1 to 2 tbsp (25 to 50 g) rose dust (see page 100)

10 drops tea tree essential oil

5 drops rose essential oil

10 drops geranium essential oil

Small jars or tins

1. Simply place dry rose petals and buds into a jar and decant your choice of oil over the roses. If you try to do oil first, then roses, you will have a mess on your hands! Seal and store in the refrigerator, allowing the oil to infuse. After 4 to 5 days, the oil can be used for various crafts including lip balms, hair treatments and this pretty salve!

2. Scoop the coconut oil and petroleum jelly into a microwave safe bowl. Heat the oil in 30-second intervals until *just melted*. Do not boil! Add in the infused rose oil and stir well until combined.

3. Stir rose dust into the mixture.

4. Add all three essential oils, using geranium as a similar rose scent at a less expensive price. Tea tree oil adds a natural boost of antiseptic.

5. Stir gently until all of the ingredients are fully incorporated and decant them immediately into small jars or tins. The salve will "harden up" just a bit as it cools, but still remains easily spreadable for the rough skin on elbows, heels, lips or elsewhere!

CRAFTING ROSE BEADS

To create rose beads, the leftover pulp of rose petals is mashed, squeezed and formed into little fragrant balls that harden into beads. The story goes that these beads were made, dried and strung onto string and used bead by bead to inspire prayer. In fact, the very name "rosary" comes from this tradition of using actual rose beads strung as an instrument of religious practice.

Rose "pulp" from extracting rosewater (see page 102)

Toothpicks

1. Once you have extracted rosewater from the petals, the leftover pulp should be strained and cooled.

2. Take small amounts of pulp in your hand, squeeze and roll them until they begin to hold together. There should be very little liquid in the pulp and none should drip from the beads.

3. Place a toothpick through each bead gently, squeezing the soft bead around the toothpick to reshape if needed.

4. Allow beads to dry for 6 to 8 days, turning the toothpicks at least once a day to keep the threading hole open.

5. Once dry, the beads are quite hard to the touch, but still maintain a pretty rose scent. String them onto your very own rosary, add them to beaded necklaces (see below), earrings or bracelets or attach to key chains.

ROSE BEAD NECKLACE

This mixed metal necklace is inspired by a classic rosary, using various metals and homemade rose beads (see above). I used jewelry wire instead of thread because the metal beads are slightly heavier and the wire helps the necklace keep its shape.

Rose beads

Copper jewelry wire

Copper necklace clasp (any kind)

Various metallic beads

Jump ring

1. Wrap the rose beads in copper wire and twist ends to secure each bead. Rose beads can look a little akin to meatballs, so the addition of the wire adds interest and reduces the "meatball" look.

2. Attach a 12- to 14-inch (30- to 35-cm) length of copper jewelry wire to a necklace clasp.

3. String various metallic beads of your choice in various patterns, interspersing copper-wrapped rose beads when desired.

4. Close the necklace by attaching the copper wire to a jump ring, then attach around the neck to necklace clasp.

CHAPTER 12

THE CUDDLIEST PLANTS—
LAMB'S EAR & SAGE

Lamb's ear is one of those plants that becomes so familiar that folks start to dismiss it. That is a shame, for lamb's ear is one of the most adorable, yet easy-to-grow plants in the garden. Known as *Stachys byzantina* to official botanists, its common name lamb's ear suits it much better. This little plant has quite possibly the softest "fur" in the garden and truly resembles a sweet little lamb's ear. Children are always drawn in by this fuzzy little plant and even full-grown adults can't help but bend down to feel it. Join me as I show you how to turn these fuzzy little ears into pretty wreaths, flower wraps and corsages!

HOW TO GROW LAMB'S EAR AND SAGE

LAMB'S EAR – STACHYS BYZANTINE

You might think a fun little plant like this would be hard to grow, but lamb's ear is completely forgiving, tough and easy to propagate. It grows into mats, covering the ground 2 to 3 inches (5 to 7.5 cm) from the surface. In summer, each plant will put up tall stalks of purple flowers and then dry erect as is. Most gardeners hate these flower stalks and cut them down quickly, but they make a fun crafting supply if you can wait until they dry in the dog days of summer. The ears themselves make great crafting materials as well and lucky for us, they grow back very quickly once cut.

GARDEN SAGE – SALVIA OFFICINALIS

Sage is lamb's ear minus the fur, plus a great taste and scent. There are many different varieties of sage, but good old Garden Sage (Salvia officinalis) is the one you want for crafting and for cooking. Sage has a similar look to lamb's ear, but differs in both feel and taste. It will fill out a pot nicely, growing wider than tall and offers a nice, soft texture to stiffer plantings like chives or iris. Sage is harvested to use in meal preparations and other "heavy" culinary dishes, but also makes a nice crafting material.

When growing sage, keep a few things in mind:

» Cut often, cut hard. Give sage a couple months to become established, but then trim your plant often to use the leaves for crafting and cooking. The plant will replenish those cut leaves easily and the constant cutting will keep the plant low to the ground and bushy.

» Sage likes it hot, but not too hot. Sage grows well in zones 5 to 8, but will die off in zone 4 winters and zone 9 summers. If you want to push your zone, plant in a cool, partially shaded zone 9 garden and mulch heavily in a zone 4 garden. Sage might just make it with a little help, but your chances are about 50/50.

» Watch the water! Sage, like many herbs, hates wet feet. Make sure the soil it is in drains well and don't go overboard watering container-planted sage.

» Preserve sage by cutting bunches and hanging upside down in a cool, dry place. Alternatively, dry leaves in a dehydrator or chop up bits and freeze in ice cubes. With a few sage plants in the garden, there is no reason you cannot have sage all winter long with these preserving methods.

PROPAGATING LAMB'S EAR AND SAGE

Propagating lamb's ear is simply a matter of dividing the plants you already have. If you have a few years, you could actually divide one single plant into many via multiplication. To divide, gently dig up your plant and note where the roots are. You are going to split up the plant, making sure each piece has a small section of roots, a stem and a pair of leaves. You can make larger divisions than this (with more roots, stems and leaves), but do not make them any smaller. Simply plant each division, water it in and unless you are experiencing a drought, the lamb's ear will do just fine on its own and you will have a carpet of lamb's ear before you know it!

Sage can be propagated via cuttings. Simply cut off a new stem that is of medium size for the plant and dip in hormone rooting powder. Place the cutting in loose potting soil and keep moist, but not wet. In a few months, roots will develop, signaling the plant is ready to move into the garden.

NOTE: Due to the easy ability to grow, divide and multiply, some consider lamb's ear a weed. It is sometimes considered invasive near lawns. I have grown lamb's ear in several different gardens in different zones and have never had a problem with it. I like the plant and enjoy the way it spreads. It is certainly nowhere near bindweed or poison ivy in growth habit, but plant with caution if you do not want it to spread.

SIMPLE LAMB'S EAR AND SAGE CRAFTS

From the leaves to the stalks, lamb's ear and sage are pretty crafting materials that can be grown inexpensively. Over the next several pages you will find crafts from the simplest to a bit more complex to get you crafting with these cuddly plants!

Fresh, large lamb's ear or sage leaves

Hot glue

Pencil or small skewer

Floral tape

Floral wire

Various forms and base foundations

Fuzzy licorice vine (optional)

FLOWERS

The leaves of lamb's ear and sage can be used for various crafts, including actual miniature lambs, but my favorite way to utilize them is to make little flowers. Use the flowers as gift toppers, decorate a pot or two or simply add to your kitchen windowsill as decoration! Note that the flowers will last a few weeks, but will not last forever, so treat them like cut flowers to be enjoyed for a short time.

ROSE

The easiest flower to make is a simple curled rose. Place a pencil or small skewer on the small edge of a leaf and twirl the leaf around creating a bloom. Hot glue the edge to secure and add a dab of glue to the center to keep from unfurling. Lamb's ear or sage both make cute rolled roses. Use the rolled piece as the centerpiece for more complicated blooms.

TULIP

Take 6 leaves and lay them in a star shape with the small ends pointed out. Hot glue the middles pieces together. Place a small plastic egg inside the flower to form it around. Gather the leaves into a tulip shape around the egg and glue on the inside to secure. Remove egg. Lamb's ear works best for this design.

(continued)

Twist the leaf to create a simple rose or the base of more intricate blooms.

SIMPLE LAMB'S EAR AND SAGE CRAFTS (CONTINUED)

OTHER FUN SHAPES

BOWS

These can be made with hot glue or wire. Both are easy! Start with two large leaves and two medium leaves, looping the large leaves tip to tip to create a loop. Alternatively, place floral wire through the ends of each and twist to secure. Attach the two small leaves as bow "ends" with glue or wire.

Top your bow with a button, small wildflower or other pretty bits!

BALLS

Create pretty, fuzzy balls by layering large leaves to a styrofoam ball. Start at the top with leaves meeting at a point, then cascading down in layers to the bottom of the ball. Attach liberally with hot glue. (See wreath technique on page 116 which can be used on balls and cones as well.)

(continued)

To create a bow, begin by folding the two loops.

Add small lamb's ear leaves to create the bow's "ends."

SIMPLE LAMB'S EAR AND SAGE CRAFTS (CONTINUED)

MIXED PLANT CORSAGE

This pretty corsage mixes lamb's ear *and* sage for a pretty contrasting texture and introduces a fuzzy licorice vine as an accent. These can be used as decorations or corsage and boutonnières bases.

1. Roll a sage leaf into a tight roll and pierce it with two pieces of floral wire into an "x." Bend lamb's ear leaves into loops and place onto the wires with the curved side facing out.

2. Squeeze the leaves into the center to form a rosette.

3. Keep the corsage tight by pinching the base and wrapping floral tape around the leaves as you build.

4. Add in as many layers of looped leaves as you wish, then fold wires down gently to form a stem. Wrap the stem in floral tape.

5. Add in accents of fuzzy licorice vine if desired. Alternatively, use the lamb's ear and sage rosette as a base for little wildflowers and other "pretties" for a new take on a traditional corsage or boutonnière.

Step 1: Create a roll and add two loops.

Step 2: Add two more loops and secure with wire.

Steps 3 & 4: Wrap the base to secure each layer of "petal" leaves.

Step 5: Licorice vine and other small accents can be added to the corsage.

SIMPLE LAMB'S EAR AND SAGE CRAFTS (CONTINUED)

LAMB'S EAR BOUQUET WRAP

If you are in the garden making a last minute bouquet, the stems can sometimes end up a bit sloppy. Lamb's ear to the rescue! Simply pick three large leaves with no blemishes, place them stem side down and wrap with a bit of twine for an instant bouquet upgrade. Liven up plain old vases with a similar wrap!

LAMB'S EAR ANGEL SKIRTS

Sometimes people are turned off of crafting because they think everything must be from scratch and take hours. That is simply not true! Updating a cheap product with natural upgrades is still crafting! It is fast, fun and your chances of success are much higher! Enter twenty-cent ornaments found on clearance after Christmas.

These little angels had darling faces, but the cone-shaped skirts had fabric on them that was just awful. Terrible color, terrible texture and ugly seaming relegated these angels to clearance. A few lamb's ear leaves later and they now have silky, fine skirts that blend beautifully with the scarves and capes already on the ornament.

Wrap a bouquet in lamb's ear for a silky soft finish.

Dress up cheap store bought decorations with luxe natural materials, like this lamb's ear skirt.

LAMB'S EAR STRAW WREATH

This wreath is made by simply layering lamb's ear leaves on a straw wreath form (dollar store!) and attaching with golden tacks (dollar store!). Mod Podge can be used to seal the leaves onto the form, but is not necessary. Once a base of leaves is formed, fuzzy licorice vine fills in any gaps and adds textural interest!

YIELD—1 WREATH

40 to 50 medium to large lamb's ear leaves

Mod Podge (optional)

Straw wreath form

Thumbtacks

Fuzzy licorice plant

Burlap ribbon

Protective spray (optional)

1. Snip leaves as low as possible along the stem. You will trim stems at the end of the project.

2. For extra security, use Mod Podge to attach leaves around the top circumference of the wreath form, curving each leaf around the form as you go. Secure each leaf at the top and bottom with a thumbtack on each.

3. Go around the wreath again, placing smaller leaves to overlap the tips of your previous circle.

4. Add licorice vine (the fuzzy variety!) to fill in holes and add textural interest! Secure with pins.

5. Knot a burlap ribbon to hang. Spray wreath with protective spray for longer-lasting leaves if you wish, but lamb's ear dries quite nicely without it and retains the full silky texture without the spray.

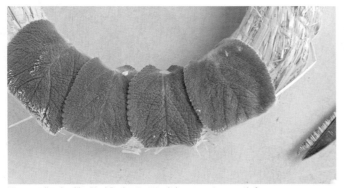
Use an adhesive like Mod Podge to attach leaves onto wreath form.

Use thumbtacks to secure leaf ends and add visual interest.

Add a layer of leaves and thumbtacks from the opposing side of the wreath for a pretty pattern.

Finish the wreath with other decorative plants such as the pictured fuzzy licorice vine.

CHAPTER 13

THE GREAT DAME OF THE VEGGIE PLOT— THE TOMATO

I remember one of the very first gifts I received as a new homeowner. It was a tomato. Actually, it was two tomatoes and put together, they were as large as my head. At first, I thought them a strange welcoming gift from our next-door neighbors, but after slicing one open, I realized that these were the crown jewels of gifts. That day, I sliced up both tomatoes, hit them with a tiny bit of shaved salt and that was my royal lunch for the day. They were divine. Those neighbors turned out to be the loveliest of people and Mr. Lyon was the one who taught me how to sacrifice the non-fruiting stems for the good of the developing tomato fruits. From that point on, I have been on a journey to grow tomatoes as well as the Lyons did, so that I may gift as well as they did.

WHICH TOMATO SHOULD I GROW?

The question *"Which tomato should I grow?"* is somewhat laughable because every tomato growing fool I know grows at least 3 to 4 different types. The really crazy ones have 20 or 30 setting fruit in their gardens! The fact is, tomatoes are the #1 homecrop grown and it is no wonder! The taste of any homegrown tomato straight off the vine versus *any* supermarket tomato is highly superior.

When you purchase tomato plants, nurseries and stores in your area are typically bringing to market tomatoes that will do well in your area. That is a plus and a jumping off point. However, you might want to check out the following suggestions from home and garden bloggers and some of the largest plant companies around. There's plenty to choose from and you might just find a new favorite!

BURPEE HOME GARDEN

» For early fruiting: Fourth of July or Early Girl (Pan-Am is coming out with Summer Girl, an improvement to Early Girl in 2016!)

» For the best burger slicing toms: Superstar Hybrid and Big Beef

» For an heirloom style: Pineapple Old Time

PAN-AMERICAN SEED

» For fun color: Chocolate Sprinkles

» For a sweet tooth: Sugar Rush Cherry Tomato

» For containers: Tiny Treats–an Indeterminate Container Cherry Tom (rare)

THE BLOGGERS

» For snacking: Kristin of That Blooming Garden (Zone 8, BC, Canada) suggests Peace Vine and Silvery Fir Tree for intense flavor and Wapsipinicon Peach as a perfect yellow tomato.

» For a short season: Kristin also suggests Stupice, first to flower in her garden!

» For a hot climate: Ally of Garden Ally suggests Juliet, which keeps on trucking through the heat!

» For resistance to nematodes: Ally says Celebrity does the best, and Jane of Cottage at the Crossroads in South Carolina agrees!

» For garden snacking: Paula of Sweet Pea Blog in Virginia says that Sungolds are the perfect off-the-vine snack.

» For canning: Paula sticks with Viva.

» For the perfect summer tomato: Jane Windham of Cottage at the Crossroads suggests heirloom Cherokee Purple for its amazing taste and Lemon Boy for a low acid yellow.

» In the Pacific Northwest: Shelley of Sow and Dipity has experience growing in a short coastal season. She recommends Black Krim, an indeterminate tom for short season folks who want tomatoes, not just plants! She also recommends San Marzano for sauces, a semideterminite classic that works well in the Pacific Northwest.

NATIVE-AMERICAN AND AMISH TOMATOES

Long before my neighbor Mr. Lyon started growing his world-class tomatoes, the Native North Americans and American Amish had a long-standing tradition of fantastic heirloom tomatoes. While the point of origin is rumored to be in Mexico, there is no clear documentation. However, there is clearly a tie between fantastic heirloom tomatoes and various North American cultures.

NATIVE-AMERICAN LINKED HEIRLOOMS

Cherokee Purple
When you think of a Native-American linked tomato, the Cherokee Purple often is first to come to mind. This tomato has a deep, dark pink flesh and a sweet, mild flavor. It is a favorite for a reason and if I had to pick one heirloom to grow for the rest of my life, Cherokee Purple would definitely be in the running.

Oaxacan Jewel
The Oaxacan tomato has ties to said region in Mexico and fruits in a delightful flattened shape with light pink and yellow color. The flavor is both sweet and acidic in equal measure. This is a rare variety, so if you are able to find seeds, grow your tomatoes and save those precious seeds for future generations!

Zapotec Pink Pleated Tomato
Also from the Oaxacan region, this is a very rare tomato with a very cool shape. When cut open, it looks almost like ribbons, or the pleats on a lady's skirt. This tomato is known to be quite "fleshy", so is often served baked instead of raw. The shape alone, though, makes it stand out from its peers.

AMISH HEIRLOOMS

The Amish have a serious catalog of heirloom hybrids. On the top of the familiarity list is most likely the Brandywine tomato, bred a hundred different ways from Sunday and all delicious. Here are a few more classic Amish heirlooms.

Red Brandywine Tomato
As a Pennsylvania 1889 heirloom, the Brandywine tomato is one of the classic heirlooms that gardeners know and love. The taste is sweet and perfect for eating sliced and sun-warmed from the garden.

Amish Mayberry Tomato
This pretty pink tomato grows fairly large and each plant produces many tomatoes. The flavor is mild, but the large harvest and pretty color make this tomato a keeper!

The Dutchman Tomato
Grown by one of the first rare seed growers, Merlin Glecker, this pink-red tomato is large and very, very sweet!
It is a shame to use Dutchmans in cooking, so save them for fresh salads, salsas and fresh munching straight off the vine.

Orange Oxheart
This orange tomato has a beautiful design on the interior when sliced, reminiscent of a heart. This particular "heart" tomato will produce fruit mid-season instead of late in the season, making it a favorite!

Josie's Amish White Tomato
For a bold tomato salsa, you might want to combine yellows and oranges with this pretty heirloom. The flesh is a very light yellow, and looks almost white at times. The fruit is large and tastes meaty, but with a light flavor.

GROWING TOMATOES—BASICS AND TIPS

A discussion of tomatoes is simply not complete without mentioning my Grannie and Grandpa's garden. Though I was too young to understand what a gift Grandpa's acre-wide garden was, I do remember a few things about his tomato technique. He was always in competition to grow the best, biggest tomato in the church and he often succeeded. To grow these giant tomatoes, he always did three things:

1. Dug a deep hole, double the width and triple the depth of the plant.

2. Added 1 cup (400 g) Epsom salt to the bottom of the hole.

3. Sprinkled alfalfa pellets on top of the soil after planting.

I use these same time-honored tips in my garden to grow both heirloom tomatoes and strong and steady hybrids. Why not try a little Epsom salt or alfalfa in your garden this season? You might be surprised at the wisdom of these old-timer standbys!

GROWING FROM SEED

Tomatoes are often grown from seed because nurseries are often lacking in variety when it comes to tomato plants. There might be 10 to 12 varieties of plants to choose from, but there are hundreds of seeds! Ordering seeds online through eBay, Amazon or independent rare seed sellers is a great way to try interesting new hybrids and old heirlooms that might be dying out of circulation.

To start a tomato seed, simply sprinkle 3 to 4 onto the surface of the soil of a small pot and water in until water comes out of the pot's drainage hole. Tomato seeds do not have to be pushed down into the soil like watermelon or sunflower seeds, but they should be making direct contact with the soil. Water daily enough to keep the soil moist, but not wet.

Once sprouts emerge, choose the best of the group to save and cut the rest of the seedlings off at the soil line with scissors. Do not pull them out as this might disturb the roots of your "choice" plant. Continue to water every other day or so, whenever the first 1 to 2 inches (2.5 to 5 cm) of soil dries out.

Once your seedling is 4 to 5 inches (10 to 13 cm) tall and strong, plant in a larger pot or garden plot in very rich, loamy soil. Place crushed eggshells around the base of the plant periodically to give extra calcium to the plant, helping it avoid blossom end rot. When you start seeing fruit develop, pluck off side shoots that are not bearing fruit in order to give the most nutrition possible to the developing tomatoes. Continue plucking throughout the plant's life.

When tomatoes are fully ripe, pluck and eat before other critters get to them. Tomatoes are a delicacy for all—especially those rascally groundhogs!

With cherry tomato plants producing new fruits daily, a determinate slicer haul or a frost on the horizon, you might have more tomatoes than you know what to do with. You might want to put those extra tomatoes to good use in crafts for the kids or fun culinary gifts for neighbors. You might even be inspired by the humble tomato's form and make the cute vintage fabric pincushions in this chapter!

TOMATOES FOR KIDS, CRAFTS AND GIFTS

Many kids love tomatoes without any persuasion whatsoever, but some need a helping hand. Have fun experimenting with various tomatoes' sizes, colors and shapes to get the kids excited about this delicious food!

TOMATO CATERPILLARS
Line up slices of cucumber, plump grapes or yellow tomatoes all in a row, topping them off with a bright red tomato. Add candy eyes, an edible markered smile and voila!

STRIPEY TOP HATS
Get out chunky cheese slices and start stacking with brightly colored tomato slices for fun little top hats! Dr. Seuss day anyone?

MUSHROOMS
Let kids carve mushroom bases out of a semi-soft white cheese and top with half a cherry tomato to make a field of fun mushrooms. Where are the fairies?

TOMATO FACE
This is such a simple, child-driven activity and it always ends up with the kids downing 2 to 3 servings of veggies! Start with a giant beefsteak, or "ugly" tomato, and make thick slices. This is your "face." Lay the face on a plate for each child and serve up a platter of noses, ears, eyes and other bits. Cashews work great for ears, almond slivers are great for teeth, pumpkin seeds make fine ears or eyes and raisins are always a welcome addition for detailing.

Create a "tomato-face" bar for kids with large sliced "faces" of tomato and other nuts and veggies for the features.

SWEET AND SOUR SUNGOLD AND PEACH PRESERVES

Once you have grown world-class tomatoes, you might want to jar up a few! This recipe is crisp, fresh, sweet and a little spicy. It pairs well with a hot biscuit or slice of whole wheat bread, but can also be used to flavor a piece of grilled pork or chicken. Whip up this recipe in bulk to give to friends and save a bunch in the pantry!

YEILD—2 TO 3 (8-OZ [237-ML]) JARS

1 ⅔ cups (290 g) fresh or frozen peaches

⅔ cup (120 g) brown sugar

2 tbsp (30 ml) quick set pectin

2 tbsp (30 ml) lemon juice

1 to 2 inch (2.5 to 5 cm) chunk of ginger, peeled

1 cup (175 g) sungold cherry tomatoes

1. Chop peaches into small chunks and mix with sugar, pectin and lemon juice in a large bowl.

2. Let the mixture stand for 10 to 12 minutes.

3. Cut the ginger into small chunks and add to a blender with the sungold tomatoes. Blend until the mixture is a fine "mush."

4. Add the tomato mixture to the peach mixture in a small pot over medium heat, and stir for 5 minutes, mashing the peaches slightly as you stir.

5. Carefully pour the mixture into sterilized canning jars. The preserves are good immediately, but are even better after having a few days to meld flavors.

NOTE: Preserves can be canned using traditional pressure-canning methods, used up immediately (yum!) or frozen once cooled.

Add tomato mixture to peach chunks.

Blend until well combined.

DIY VINTAGE FABRIC TOMATO PINCUSHIONS

The classic tomato pincushion is a perennial favorite, but why not update the look with pretty vintage fabrics and muted felt toppers? Try pink, blues, yellows, purples and even greens for a fun twist on the classic red pincushion! This simple little craft makes a sweet gift for the sewist in your family and is a fun little craft that older kids can enjoy on snowy winter evenings when fresh tomatoes are nothing but a dream. There are plenty of tutorials for pincushions on the web, but most require many, many steps. I have broken this project down for you into the simplest form possible, so even beginner sewists can accomplish this craft!

Various pretty thrifted fabrics

Needle and thread

Stuffing such as linen bits, cotton stuffing and wool

Thick embroidery floss

Green felt

Fabric scissors

Fabric glue

1. Cut a rectangle of fabric. 6 x 3 inches (15 cm x 7.5 cm) is a good place to start, but yours can be larger or smaller.

2. Fold the fabric in half, right side in and make a running stitch along both sides. Run a few stitches back through the "accordion pleats" for stability and knot to secure. You will have two rouched sides.

3. Turn material back out so that your stitches are hidden inside and the right side of the fabric is facing out. It will look like a little basket.

4. Stuff your tomato. I use old linen napkins that are stained, cut them into small bits, then add cotton balls around the edges to minimize any lumpiness.

5. Sew the top shut, knotting to secure. This section will be hidden by the topper.

6. With a thick embroidery floss, wrap the tomato, tightly creating little sections like you see in a fat, heirloom style tomato. Secure with knots at the top where your topper will go.

7. Cut your tomato topper from crafting felt with fabric scissors. Attach with glue to the top of the tomato, covering up all those stitches and knots!

NOTE: This simple pattern can be switched up to make cute little pumpkins as well! Simply use thrifted velvet or sweater wool for the pumpkin instead of cotton and add a stem in place of tomato topper!

DID YOU KNOW? The original pincushions in the 1300s and 1400s were called "pin-poppets." Can we bring that back please?

DID YOU KNOW? The cute little strawberry hanging off the classic tomato pincushion is filled with emery in order to clean and sharpen needles.

DID YOU KNOW? The tomato is a sign of good luck. In fact, tomatoes used to be set upon mantles to bless a household, but would then rot. Clever housewives started creating little stuffed tomatoes to replace them. Of course, they made a smart place to stick a needle or two that you wouldn't want to lose! The tomato pincushion was born!

DID YOU KNOW? The Victorians arguably had the best tomato pincushion collections. One was certainly not enough and the Victorian ladies prided themselves on having a lovely little grouping of these tchotchkes!

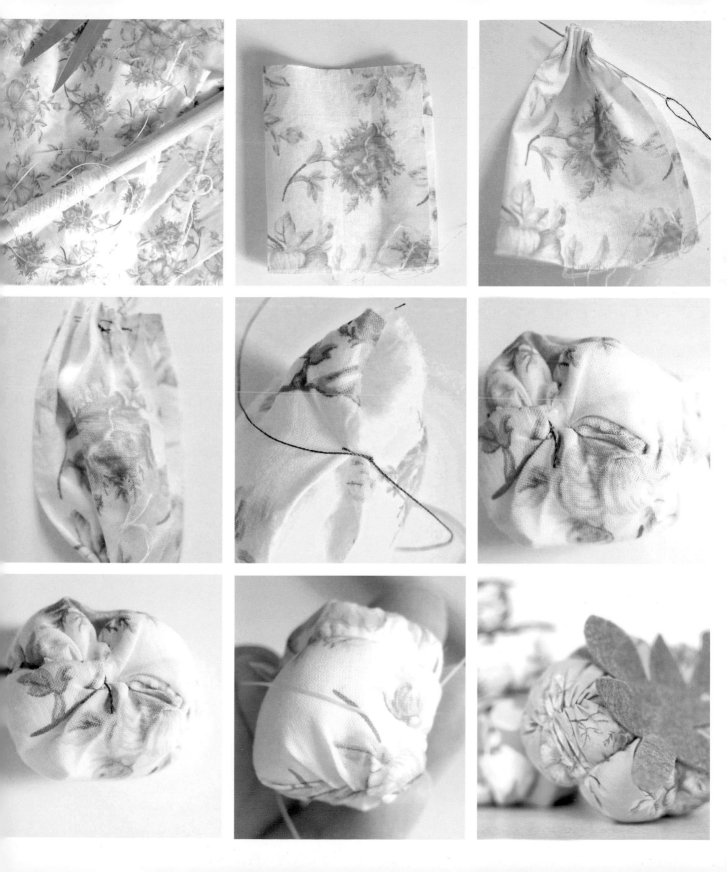

GINGER PICKLED TOMATOES

You may have canned a few pecks of pickled peppers, but have you ever put up a few pickled tomatoes? If you have more tomatoes than you know what to do with, this is the recipe for you! These are crisp and fresh, lending themselves to be a perfect complement for rich and meaty dishes. Consider these an alternative to the ubiquitous pickle and serve with pork sliders, burgers and even chili. This recipe works best with a firm tomato, such as a Roma, but can also be made with *any* green tomato! This recipe calls for "pickle crisp granules" which eliminate the need for pickling lime and the pre-soak process.

YIELD—ONE 1-QUART (946-ML) JAR

1 (1-quart [946-ml]) canning jar

3 tbsp (45 g) of sliced ginger

5 to 6 Roma tomatoes (or equivalent green tomatoes)

¼ tsp pickle crisp granules

2 tbsp (30 g) salt

5 tbsp (75 g) brown sugar (essential!)

2 tbsp (30 g) mustard seeds

1 ½ cups (354 ml) apple cider vinegar

Hot water (if needed)

1. Sterilize the jar, rinse and dry.

2. Cut the ginger into small slivers and the tomatoes into bite-sized chunks.

3. Add the ginger, pickle crisp granules, salt, sugar and mustard seeds to the jar. Cover with the vinegar and shake.

4. Add the chunks of tomato until the jar is ⅚ full.

5. Pour hot water over the top if needed to fill. Leave 1 inch (2.5 cm) of space at the top of the jar. Seal and shake.

6. Use the pressure-canning method to store for long periods of time or simply seal and store in the fridge for a small batch.

section five

GATHERED FROM THE GROCERY AISLES

This section is going to appeal to you at two very different extremes. You will either be in the depths of a cold and dreary winter and crave some tropicals like mad or you will be luxuriating under a summer sun down South and notice how many wasted oranges are falling to the ground uneaten. You will hasten to scoop up those grapefruits and oranges and lemons and limes and dry them as quick as the sun can shine to make beautiful, lasting garlands, ornaments and light catchers. You might make a few sugar scrubs with exotic scents or work up a dozen or so jars of my famous coconut whips. Perhaps stick with simple flavored salts or sugars. Note that the mixtures are loose recipes that can be thickened or thinned depending on your preferences. Most can be scented with your choice of essential oils or you can use my recipes exactly. Flexibility and creativity are allowed here!

The projects in this section are some of my favorites and they are perfect for the tropical residents who have access to buckets of ingredients from the trees and fields. They are also perfect for those of us stuck in a cold house this winter who can make it to a grocery store to stock up before the next snowstorm. Just grab a few extra bags of sugar, a few bags of citrus and an extra tin of coffee and prepare for a kitchen that smells like the beach!

CHAPTER 14

CRAFTY CITRUS

Lemons, limes, grapefruits and oranges are the jewels of the fruit world. Full of zesty flavor and beautiful colors, they are as beneficial to our bodies as they are to our crafting pantry. Join me as I show you how to grow these everyday citrus fruits, then turn them into pretty garlands, lightcatchers and a fantastic little lotion bar!

HOW TO GROW CITRUS IN A POT

In my zone 6 garden, I am quite limited when it comes to citrus. Sure, I can hit up the grocery store for just about anything I need, but if I want to grow my own, I have to grow it in a pot. Meyer Lemons, Key Limes and other small citrus trees are the ticket for colder zone gardeners, while you lucky folks in warmer locales can grow any citrus you darn well please in your backyard. Oranges, lemons, grapefruits and limes are yours for the picking!

If you are stuck growing citrus in a pot, here is what you need to know. You can start a citrus plant from seed, but it takes 2 to 3 years to get the plant to a mature size and then to fruiting. Commercial sellers also graft their trees onto hardy root stock, creating a tree that is strong and tough, yet that produces desirable traits in its fruits. Follow their lead and start with a small grafted tree with a year of growth already on it. Plant your citrus tree in the largest pot and richest soil that you can afford. Though these are small trees, they are still *trees*. They need plenty of room to put down roots and plenty of nutrition to actually fruit. Here are some additional tips to keep your citrus plant happy.

» **Give them light!** Think about the native growing grounds of citrus trees. Think about how badly skin may burns when visiting those native stomping grounds. Citrus trees love light and they are bred to thrive on it. A greenhouse or atrium is best, but a large southern facing window might also work.

» **Take them outside!** When the weather permits, roll that pot out to the porch and let it soak up the sun! Once the thermometer hits 50°F (10°C), you are safe to roll that citrus tree outdoors, but keep an eye on nighttime temperatures. If the temperature is dipping below 40°F (4.4°C), it is safer to roll the pot back in at night. I know, I know. That is a lot of work. How delightful are those fresh lemons picked from the tree this morning, though? Once the temperature stays above 50°F (10°C) at night, give your citrus trees a sunny spot outside and enjoy the harvest.

» **Wheels.** Did you notice that I said "roll" in the previous tip? If you have followed instructions and planted your tree in a large pot with rich soil, it will be incredibly heavy. A wheeled pot or small rolling bottom for your pot is necessary.

» **Water, but not too much.** You can easily overwater potted plants, so your rule of thumb is to make sure the soil is moist, but not sopping wet. I water ½ gallon (2 L) twice a week, but adjust based on whether the soil has dried out or not. Listen to your plants! If the soil is wet (not just moist) leave it be! If you can get the plant outside and into the sun, *do it*. The sun and wind will help dry out an over-watered plant. Think of your plants as your belly. You know that awful feeling when you have drunk too much water much too quickly and it slushes around in your stomach? When plants have wet (not moist, but *wet*) soil, they have "slushy belly." Stick to enough water to keep their "throat" from getting dry, but not so much that they are waterlogged. It can ultimately spell death for many plants.

» **Fertilize.** Apply a slow-release granular fertilizer high in nitrogen once a month and make certain that your tree receives 6 to 8 hours of sunlight a day.

NOTE: Prune for shape anytime indoors and prune all suckers that grow beneath the graft, which looks like a small scar on the stem. The suckers are new trees attempting to grow from the less desirable root stock and will steal nutrients and energy from the tree you are attempting to grow and fruit.

DIY DRIED CITRUS ORNAMENTS, GARLANDS AND LIGHT CATCHERS

If you are successful growing your own citrus, or if you are one of the lucky few who have wild citrus growing in the backyard, then pick a few that are not perfect and bring them inside for crafting. Save the perfect ones to *eat*! Those of you without your own tree might check out the "seconds" at your local grocery store or farmer's market. There are often various fruits with slightly damaged skins or bruises that will work just fine for crafting and cost a fraction of the price.

My favorite citrus for creating ornaments, garlands and light catchers is the under-appreciated grapefruit. With a scent that is a little bit sweet and a little bit sharp, it is citrusy without being overbearingly so. The pink grapefruits also boast the most amazing color that complements décor from Christmas all the way through Valentine's Day. Oranges, lemons and limes also look great at Christmastime, but I also like them for summer décor with the fresh colors and scents. All of these fruits are cut thinly on a mandolin so that the insides are translucent and look brilliant when backlit in a window or on a fireplace mantel. A vertical garland from a doorframe or window, a garland around a tree or a singular light catching slice or two in the kitchen window bring brightness to dull winter landscapes and offer fresh scents to stuffy homes.

Various citrus fruits such as grapefruit, lemon or orange

Mandolin or kitchen knife

Oven or dehydrator

Sheet pan

Large craft needle and string

VARIATION: VERTICAL CITRUS GARLANDS

To create a vertical garland, you are simply going to make small "stacks" of citrus slices spread along a length of string. The process follows the same steps as a horizontal garland, but instead of knotting each slice individually, string 4 to 5 pieces in a group, then tie a large knot in the string. Once hung, these periodic knots create "stops" where slices stack upon each other. Hang from hooks, in corners of the room or anywhere that needs a bit of vertical interest!

1. Carefully cut up your citrus into thin slices, using a kitchen knife or mandolin.

2. Place the slices into a dehydrator, on a sheet pan in a sunny window or in your oven at its lowest temperature to dry. The oven works the fastest, the window is the slowest and the dehydrator does the best job of getting them incredibly dry. If you do not get the slices dry enough, they will start to develop mold after several weeks. To avoid mold completely, use a dehydrator.

3. Using a large craft needle, threaded with string, pierce the flesh of the fruit when it is 80 to 90 percent dry. When the fruit is completely dry, it can become brittle. When it still has a bit of moisture to it, it will keep its shape but remain flexible enough to thread. Thread the citrus slice and knot at the top. You have successfully made a citrus ornament! Make a collection and hang from the branches of your Christmas tree or simply hang a few ornaments from a window to catch the light!

4. For garlands, you are basically going to make a long strand of ornaments. Thread a long string onto a large craft needle 12 inches (30 cm) longer than the length of garland you plan to make. (Garlands are typically from 4 to 12 feet [1 to 4 m] or longer). Lay out your citrus slices to create a pleasing arrangement and line them up along your string. Adjust spacing accordingly.

5. To thread, pierce the fruit slice on the farthest end of the garland and pull the string all the way through, leaving a tail of 6 inches (15 cm). Loop the thread around the back of the fruit again and knot at the top of the slice. This will secure the slice from wandering up and down the string once the garland is complete. Leave 1 to 2 inches (2 to 5 cm) of space and string, then knot your next citrus slice. Continue until your garland is complete!

NOTE: When slicing citrus, there are two "designs" that can result depending on the way you slice the fruit. If you slice from tip to tip (where the fruit hung from the tree), you will see curved ribs vertically up and down the fruit. If you cut across the fruit, however, you will see the classic sunburst citrus design.

CITRUS LOTION BAR DIY

What is a lotion bar? I'm glad you asked! Like soap, a lotion bar is basically a hard bar made out of moisturizing ingredients. At room temperature the bar is completely solid, but when rubbed between your hands, the bar warms up just enough for a thin layer of moisturizer to coat your hands. We will start with a simple recipe that accepts a variety of different citrus scents with ease. For this particular project, we will be using essential oils that are commercially pressed as the result is far superior to any DIY attempt.

YIELD—20 SMALL SQUARES

1 cup (400 g) beeswax pellets

1 cup (500 g) shea butter

1 cup solid or ½ cup liquid (118 ml) coconut oil

Microwave-safe bowl or small crafting crockpot for melting

20 drops total of orange, lemon, lemongrass or grapefruit essential oils

Oiled molds

1. Place the beeswax pellets, shea butter and coconut oil into a microwave-safe bowl or small crafting crockpot.

2. Melt slowly, stirring often. The oil and butter melt much faster than the beeswax. Take your time and continue to melt at a low temperature. The beeswax *will* melt and incorporate! *Do not allow the mix to boil.* This will change the chemical makeup of the soap and it can explode.

3. Add 20 drops of your favorite citrus essential oil or a combination of oils. Remember to keep the total to 20 drops. Once the mixture is completely liquid and no solid bits remain, give the mix another gentle stir and slowly pour into molds. My favorite mold for this bar and other bar soaps is a square silicone brownie baking mold. Note that the liquid is very hot, so please wear gloves if you are working with hot lotion for the first time. If you spill any little bits, they will solidify quickly. Simply peel them off the counter top or side of the bowl and remelt.

4. Allow the bars to fully harden. You may then use immediately! No waiting period required!

DID YOU KNOW? All lotion bar recipes in this book substitute for lip balms easily! Just add an extra ½ cup (118 ml) of your softer oil like olive oil or coconut oil to the mixture and use lip balm containers or tubes instead of molds. Try these luxurious moisturizers on your lips, hands and feet or all over!

NOTE: When making these bars, note that you can substitute various essential oils and even combine different scents, as long as you keep the total drops to 20 per batch. Also note that I suggest beeswax pellets as opposed to slabs. The beeswax melts very slowly compared to the coconut oil and shea butter. A slab would take a long time to melt, while the pellets are faster. Don't try to omit the beeswax completely though because it provides the structure to the bar that makes it solid at room temperature!

CHAPTER 15

COCONUT, COFFEE & OTHER TROPICALS

Welcome to the tropical chapter! Ironic considering I am writing this in the midst of a winter blizzard. I live in zone 6 where tropical plants are something to enjoy for a few months in summer or indoors in winter. I can plant pineapple tops and enjoy a houseplant, but I will never have enough light and heat to get an *actual* pineapple. Coconut, mango, jade, aloe, canna, coffee and sugar are plants that grow prolifically throughout tropical regions, but they will never grow outdoors in mine. You might be the same. However, I know some folks reading this book will be living where they *can* plant a coffee plant or harvest coconuts from the jungle. This chapter is for *you*! This chapter is also for those who live in the coldest of zones because, lucky for you, all the supplies are accessible via the grocery store or online shops for a fair price. Let's dive right in, because baby it is *cold* outside and I need to smell the scents of coconut and coffee!

HOW TO GROW GIFTABLE TROPICALS—CANNA, JADE, COFFEE AND COCONUT!

I am picking two very easy-to-grow plants to get you started with plants outside of your zone. Cannas will rot in the winter ground zones 7 and colder. Think Tennessee and on up North as a rough guide for zone 7 and up. Most Southern states range from zones 8–10. Whether you are in a cold zone or a warm zone, you *can* grow cannas. They grow very quickly and rhizomes planted in spring will grow into stems, leaves and flowers by the end of summer. If you are zone 8 and up, those cannas can stay in the ground, but colder zones need to pull them up each fall.

GROWING CANNA RHIZOMES

You might think of a rhizome as a "bulb" or "root" even though they are neither of those things. Cannas grow so easily because the rhizome is actually a horizontal stem of a plant chock full of growing material. As soon as you give the rhizome soil, warmth and water, it is ready to go! Once planted, several stems and leaves will emerge from each piece of rootstock (that bulbous looking rhizome) and grow rapidly.

HOW DO I PLANT THEM?

First things first, do *not* plant cannas until you are absolutely certain there will not be a frost. Frost will kill cannas and the rhizomes will rot in the ground almost instantly. You can check the last frost date based upon your plant hardiness zone. Cannas will not take off growing until it is 50°F (10°C) or so anyway, so planting them early does nobody any good. Hold off planting until it is starting to feel a tiny bit like summer outside! Typically, when you receive the canna rhizomes, the green stems are already emerging. If you do not see green stems, look for "eyes" or little knobs on the rhizome. Plant the rhizome with those green stems or eyes facing up towards the sun and only plant 2–3 inches (5–10 cm) deep. If your soil is very thick and clay-like, you might want to loosen the soil under your planting hole, down to 12 inches (30 cm) or so. However, cannas are tough as nails and I have never had to loosen the soil for them. They are fantastic beginner plants because they will grow pretty much anywhere! In fact, once the plant puts down roots, those roots are thick and tough, like little worms, and will help loosen the soil *for* you to plant weaker rooted plants.

Once the cannas are in the ground, give them a good watering or let the rain do its thing. Cannas will rot in the ground if you give them too much water though, so after an initial soaking, leave them be.

GROWING AND STORING CANNAS

Within a couple weeks of planting, those green stems will emerge from the soil (considering that you waited until it was warm to plant and they have received water!) and several months after that the cannas will flower. They will do all of this without any help from you. If you are experiencing drought conditions, you might water them every two weeks or so, but in zone 5 and 6 gardens, my cannas have done fine without any intervention from me.

Once they finish flowering, the canna plants will eventually turn brown and fall over. *That* is the time to "pull" them. If you wait you will have two small problems. One, the rhizomes are much harder to pull once the stem is weak or gone. Two, you will forget where the cannas are.

The cannas might also rot in the ground if you wait too long and a surprise freeze comes along. Remember, these plants are meant for the tropics! When those stems turn brown, simply grasp the stem at the bottom near the soil and pull up gently. The entire plant, roots, rhizome and all should come straight out of the ground. If your soil is very, very heavy and thick, you might have to use a shovel and dig from under the rhizome, but I have always simply pulled them out.

Once they are out of the ground, you will notice that the rhizomes have grown substantially. You can cut those rhizome pieces up next spring, much like you did with potatoes in Chapter 8, to create new plants. For now though, store your cannas in a dark, cool (not cold!) and very dry place. My basement is perfect where it hovers right around 50°F (10°C). The plants will not start to grow at that low temperature, but will also not rot. The key to keeping cannas over the winter is to make sure they do not rot or dry out. I know those are on opposite side of the spectrum, and many folks recommend storing them in sand or potting soil, but I have had the best success simply storing them in a pot or bucket and leaving them alone.

While I have thrown quite a bit of information at you about cannas, I want to reinforce that they are a *very* easy plant to start with.

CRAFTING WITH CANNAS

Canna leaves are a great crafting material, similar to hosta leaves and elephant ears. They are large and tough, making them great choices for molding cement stepping stones, wrapping vases of flowers or creating a tropical tablescape! Cannas make lovely little hostess gifts all summer long when planted by individual rhizomes in small pots in spring. Another favorite gifting tropical of mine is the similarly tough-as-nails Jade.

GROWING JADE

Jade is a succulent, such as sedum or cactus, storing plenty of water in its leaves to keep it going during times of little rainfall. They are native to southern Africa where they grow wild, sometimes into tree-like plants. Therefore, growing them in the Midwest United States means growing them indoors. There are two basics to growing a jade or money plant: *do not* overwater and *give jade light*!

If you think about Africa, those two growing requirements make sense, right? If you have a southern facing window, that sill will be the best place for your jade plant to grow in the winter. Once summer comes around, your jade plants can enjoy the sun and breezes outdoors.

PROPAGATING JADE

My favorite aspect of jade plants is their ability to propagate, or grow into new plants, very easily. You can simply pick leaves off at the stem and plant them directly into potting soil. Within a few months, that little stem and leaf will grow more tiny little leaves and solid roots and is ready to gift to your friends! This tough little plant is easy to grow in small containers as it does not need much water and the roots can grow to fill the small space with no harm done. If you are afraid of propagating plants on your own, jade is a wonderful place to start!

Though there are many different varieties of jade, all propagate the same. However, there are always new plants coming to market and many are patented. Before you propagate a plant, make certain that it is not currently under patent. Common jade is currently not under patent. Jade is a great gifting plant because it does not need tons of root room and can fit into small handmade clay or concrete planters, small hollowed out tree stumps or hanging planters. Before you tackle the more difficult tropical, jade is a great beginner tropical to get started with!

If you have success with cannas and jade, you might want to try growing tough stonecrops or branch out to try a small palm tree. There are plenty of tropicals to choose from and most make great houseplants if you can simply give them light! Once you feel confident with growing plants out of zone, you might take on the challenge of growing the more difficult tropicals such as vanilla or pineapple. If you are extraordinarily courageous, you might even try growing your very own coffee tree indoors.

WHERE DO I BUY TROPICAL PLANTS?

I love supporting local greenhouses, especially when the houses themselves are open to the public. However, I am not opposed to buying plants at a big box store or online. Canna rhizomes are available everywhere in spring, but you will be limited in color and style by shopping at Lowes, Home Depot or Walmart. Try catalogs for really interesting cannas. Cannas will go on steep discount mid-summer and I always stock up on any pretty ones and simply store them until the following summer. If you would like to simply try growing 1 to 2 cannas, ask a neighbor friend where you see them growing. Gardeners are very generous people and a basic red canna is a gift any gardener is willing to give! The best price I have found on jade is at IKEA. However, often greenhouse plants will be very inexpensive in the late winter as stores make room for spring plants. Plenty of labeled "houseplants" are simply tropical plants. Plant them outdoors in summer to help revive them and then re-pot in fall for winter gifting.

GROWING COFFEE

A coffee plant is not a difficult plant to grow, but it *is* a difficult plant to get coffee from indoors. If you are not living in a tropical zone, you most likely will be gathering *your* coffee from the grocery store. However, that doesn't mean you cannot enjoy a coffee *plant*. The hardest part of growing a coffee plant is finding a good source for the seed. From a fresh plant, you can use the coffee cherry (with seeds inside) or buy fresh seeds with the parchment (pergamino) still attached. Processed green seeds will be very hard to sprout and typical roasted coffee beans will be impossible. You can find these seeds from specialized seed providers online or by harvesting off a friend's coffee tree.

Alternatively, you will sometimes see small coffee trees for sale at local nurseries, often in the houseplant section. This is by far the best way to get started! A coffee plant needs filtered light. It grows on the jungle edge, much like the flowering dogwoods and redbuds in Eastern U.S. forests. Soil must stay moist, but not wet and a light fertilizer once a month will be fine. If you grow your coffee plant indoors, it will appreciate being rolled outdoors in summer for a little fresh air.

GROWING A COCONUT PALM

Palms are another tropical that make a pretty indoor houseplant and you can grow one straight from the coconut! Before we begin, I must be honest with you. You will not be able to get a coconut by growing a palm indoors. In fact, your coconut palm will most likely last just a couple of seasons and then putter out. However, if you live in zone 10 and up, you have the perfect conditions for growing a palm outdoors! Northerners, feel free to enjoy the process of sprouting a coconut, but for a long-lived indoor plant, you might try other members of the palm family such as the Areca Palm or palm lookalikes such as the Ponytail Palm.

If you decide to sprout a palm from seed, you will need a fresh coconut straight from a neighbor's tree, local farmer's market or from a walk on the beach. Processed coconuts in the grocery store will not do. Bury a fresh coconut in peat moss until it is halfway covered and keep it moist, but not wet. Leave it to sprout in this manner for up to a year. There is enough nutrition in the nut to keep it growing, so you shouldn't need to fertilize. After a year, plant your sprouting palm in a high sun environment and make sure it receives a good watering every other day. Palms grow about several feet each year and within 5 to 7 years, you can start looking out for coconuts.

WHAT IS MY ZONE?

The best way to find your zone is to ask a gardening neighbor. While your city might be a particular zone, your garden might be in a microclimate that is slightly warmer or cooler than the average. Your gardening neighbor will have more information via experience than any chart or graph. To get a basic idea of your zone, check out the USDA Plant Hardiness Map or Google "Plant Hardiness Map" for your country. The zones are fairly consistent across latitudinal lines, but mountains, oceans and other topographical features can change the zone dramatically. As a general guide, most of the Southern states in the US are zones 8 to 9 with Florida reigning as the Tropical Queen with zones of 10 in the Southernmost cities. Much of the Midwest is zone 4 to 6 with the plains of Nebraska being much harsher than the mountainous valleys of Pennsylvania. The Northern New England states and up into Canada can range all the way down into zone 2 to 3.

DIY COCONUT OIL

Coconut oil is all the rage right now, and though the cost has come down significantly, it is still expensive. If you live in a tropical zone where coconuts are constantly falling and denting your car, you might as well make your own! Northerners, you can also play along by using grocery store coconuts!

YIELD—1 CUP (218 G)

3 to 4 green fresh coconuts or husked coconuts

Hammer, chisel, machete and knife

Vegetable peeler

Blender

Cheesecloth

Large bowl, non-reactive (glass, ceramic or stainless steel)

Coconut oil solidifies at 76°F (24°C), but will turn from a solid to a liquid instantly when rubbed onto your skin!

1. First things first; you must gather your supplies. Coconuts straight from the tree look a bit different than the ones you see at the grocery store. They are still in a protective husk that must be stripped. Shake the husked coconut and listen for a sloshing noise. This indicates that the coconut inside is fresh. There will be a heavy side and a light side of the coconut husk, with the heavier side being rounded and possibly green. The lighter side is pointier and often light brown.

2. Using a hammer and chisel or the claw side of the hammer, attack the "light" side of the coconut. Pull the husk away and continue beating the life out of the husk until you are able to release the "hairy" brown coconut from the heavy side of the husk. Note that when I say attack, I mean attack. Remember Tom Hanks in *Castaway* with the coconut? They are a very tough nut to crack and you must use force and good aim. Be careful not to hurt yourself.

3. You now have a hairy brown coconut and if you are using coconuts from the grocery store, you will start the tutorial here! Rinse the coconut with water and then use a chisel and hammer, machete or knife to crack the coconut around the circumference. This inside nut can be cracked with one good swing of a machete, unlike the outer husk.

4. Bake the coconut halves in a 350°F (180°C) oven for 20 minutes to help separate the meat from the outer shell.

5. Cool, then pop the white meat out of the shell. Peel any brown off with a vegetable peeler.

6. Cut into chunks, then blend in a heavy-duty blender. Add little bits of water as needed to blend. The mixture should be very smooth, like a fruit smoothie.

7. Pour mixture through cheesecloth into a large, non-reactive bowl. Squeeze cheesecloth to remove all moisture from the meat.

8. Use the meat as shredded coconut at this point, or freeze it for later. If you do not really like coconut meat, throw it in the compost!

9. The liquid mixture in the bowl needs to sit overnight for the solids to separate from the liquids. Cover with plastic film and place in the refrigerator overnight. In the morning, the top will be white and ready to scoop off. That is your coconut oil!

NOTE: A green coconut, just starting to turn brown, is perfectly ripe and will be relatively easy to open with a machete. As the coconut turns brown, it becomes harder to open, but is still edible. A brown, light coconut with no green has gone bad.

COFFEE AND COCONUT SOAP BARS

There are a few things I would really hate to live without and topping the list is my morning (and afternoon!) coffee. While coffee makes a delicious drink, it also makes a pretty wonderful craft supply. Remember those beautiful filter flowers from Chapter 6? Without coffee, those flowers would have been too bright and pink, without a rich earthiness to them that real flowers have when they naturally dry. In this chapter, we use both brewed coffee and coffee grounds to create beautiful and delightful soap bars. To complement our tropical coffee, coconut gets added to the mix as well. In fact, the addition of a little coconut oil adds a light scent and a wonderful bit of moisturizer to the soap, making it a favorite all year round. The coconut oil also performs a little trick in this recipe that makes it work double duty as a moisturizer and soap.

YIELD—15 TO 20 (2-INCH [5-CM]) SQUARE SOAPS

1 lb (456 g) suspended soap base

1 cup (230 g) solid or ½ cup (118 ml) liquid coconut oil, homemade (see page 140) or store bought

Microwave-safe bowl or small crafting crockpot

2 heaping tbsp (11 g) used or fresh coffee grounds

Up to 3 tbsp (45 ml) brewed dark coffee

Oiled molds (traditional soap molds, oven-safe ceramic or glass dishware or silicone cookware)

1. Place the suspended soap base and coconut oil in a microwave-safe bowl or small crafting crockpot.

2. Melt the soap and oil 30 seconds at a time in the microwave, stirring often. Alternatively, melt in crockpot or microwave until the mix is completely liquid. *Do not allow the mix to boil. This will change the chemical makeup of the soap and it can explode.*

3. Mix in the coffee grounds and brewed coffee. Do not add more than 3 tablespoons (45 ml) as it will create too "loose" of a mix and the soap will have a hard time solidifying. Stir to combine all ingredients. The oil will begin to rise to the top.

4. Carefully decant the hot, liquid soap mixture into your oiled molds. Be careful! Allow the mixture to sit until fully hardened.

5. Once it is fully hardened, you will see the coconut oil's little "trick." It rises to the surface in this recipe, creating a layer of bright white against the dark coffee with suspended grounds. This soap will exfoliate and clean, but also provide the benefits of a lotion bar with that moisturizing layer of coconut oil. Fun, right?

NOTE: To get the look of the coffee grounds "floating" in the soap, you must use a "suspended" soap base. It simply means that the soap will suspend various hard ingredients throughout the soap instead of letting it settle on the bottom. I get mine from Stephenson's Personal Care, but it is available from many suppliers. If you do not use the suspended soap base, your soap will work the same way, but the coffee grounds will sink to the bottom of the mold. My Gardener's Allspice Scrubbing Soap (at A Nest for All Seasons) uses a plain glycerin base and the sunken layer of solids is quite beautiful.

You can also decide how dark you want the soap to be based on how much liquid coffee you place in the soap. The grounds alone will darken the soap, but up to 3 tablespoons (45 ml) of liquid coffee give the soap a deep brown coffee color (shown in photograph).

COCONUT WHIP—THREE VARIATIONS

Coconut oil has gotten a lot of attention in recent years, mainly due to its health benefits. While using coconut oil in cooking is healthful, using it for homemade lotions, balms, bars and sticks is much more up my alley. Lucky for us crafters, the popularity of coconut oil for cooking has led to a sharp decrease in price and readily available coconut oil in your local grocery store or club store. I recently saw a nice big tub of it at Sam's Club for $10!

Coconut oil is packaged in jars, rather than bottles as it is a solid at room temperature. This adds a nice solidity to loose toiletries and also allows for easy melting products, such as the lotion bars below. A good place to start with coconut oil is to learn how to make very basic "whips". Mixed with a small amount of "loose" oil like olive oil, the coconut oil loses some of its stiffness to create a nice moisturizer.

BEACH-IN-A-JAR COCONUT WHIP

This was the first coconut whip I created and it is still one of my favorites. The natural, light coconut smell of the oil blends with the "Day at the Beach" scent beautifully. This creamy coconut oil moisturizer has the smell of the beach without an overwhelming coconut scent, and it goes on like buttah. This coconut oil moisturizer is not a typical lotion that you might put on your hands. Rather, it is a thick oil that is perfect for your skin after a long bath, or perhaps even while at the beach. I love to take a little dab of it for the back of my neck or forearms where I can smell that deliciousness all day long.

Let's hop into the kitchen shall we? This simple DIY coconut oil moisturizer takes no more than 5 minutes to prep and is the perfect project to complete while waiting for the pasta water to boil.

YIELD—4 (4-OZ [118-ML]) JARS

2 cups (459 g) solid or 1 cup (236 ml) liquid coconut oil, homemade (see page 140) or store bought

¼ cup (59 ml) olive oil

"Day at the Beach" scent (from Consumercrafts.com) or other coconut scent

Stand or handheld mixer

Small quilted jars with lids

White muslin, burlap or scrap cloth for gifting

Baker's twine

1. Warm up coconut oil in the microwave, just 10 seconds at a time until it goes from a solid to liquid.

2. Add the oil to the mixing bowl with the olive oil and 15 to 20 drops of your beachy fragrance oil.

3. Begin with the mixer on the lowest setting, otherwise the liquid oil will go everywhere. You want to incorporate a lot of air into the oil, so as soon as the oils have mixed and start to cool, go ahead and crank up the speed a few notches. Keep it whipping until your coconut oil moisturizer starts to show distinct peaks (see below).

4. Now you will want to carefully ladle the coconut oil moisturizer into your little jelly jars.

5. If you wish to add a topper to your coconut oil moisturizer jar, simply cut a circle of muslin, burlap or scrap fabric about 1 inch (2.5 cm) wider than your lid.

6. Tie the string around the top rim very tightly, then slide it down over the lip of the lid to secure.

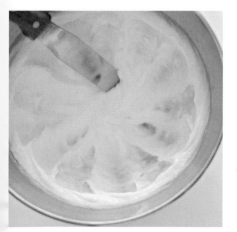

When the mixture starts to make peaks like these, it is whipped properly!

MY COCONUT OIL WON'T HARDEN UP AGAIN? WHAT DID I DO WRONG?

Nothing! You just need to keep at it! You might not have let your mixer go long enough or your work environment is too warm. Try placing the bowl in the refrigerator for 15 to 20 minutes and whip again. During winter in Pennsylvania, I could simply whip things up on my kitchen counter straight from liquid to solid. In our kitchen in Puerto Rico, I had to chill the mixture to have success!

SHEA AND COCONUT FALL WHIP

This DIY lotion is similar to my summer Beach-in-a-Jar Coconut Whip (page 145), but is a little more substantial, yellow in color and smells like fall! The base is coconut oil and shea butter found at bulk food stores, specialty groceries or online. I buy mine at Amazon or Costco. The process for this DIY lotion is slightly more involved than the basic coconut beach whip, but similar.

YIELD—4–5 (4-OZ [118-ML]) JARS

2 cups (459 g) coconut oil, plus more if needed

8 oz (227 g) yellow shea butter

Stand or handheld mixer

20 to 25 drops of pumpkin or other fall scent essential oil

Canning jars for storage

1. Start with the solid coconut oil and shea butter and melt it down very slowly. *Do not boil.* I use my microwave and go 10 to 30 seconds at a time until the solids turn mostly liquid. A small crafting crockpot also works. The mixture looks gross at first until the two oils completely mix and air is whipped into the concoction. Do not be scared off by the look of the mixture at the beginning.

2. When you see small chunks of shea butter that are very soft from being melted, but not completely liquid, that is fine. Better slightly solid than to go too far and boil the oil. Let your mixer go on level 1 or 2 until the mixture starts to take on a uniform yellow color with small bits of shea still visible.

3. When the mixture just slightly holds to a spoon, you can bump the mixer speed up to 3 to 4, or medium. Keep increasing the whipping speed as more air incorporates into the mixture and it becomes less sloppy and liquid. You will finish on the highest whip setting available.

4. It will take 10 minutes or more to get the consistency of whipped icing for your DIY lotion. If you want the mix thicker, you can add some more liquid coconut oil at this point along with your 20 to 25 drops of fragrance oil. Whip to incorporate.

5. Dispense the mixture into your jars and allow it to "harden up" a bit over the next couple of days.

Step 2: Shea butter takes longer to melt down and incorporate, so small chunks at first are okay.

Step 3: A mixture that holds loosely to a spoon indicates that the mixture is ready to whip more quickly.

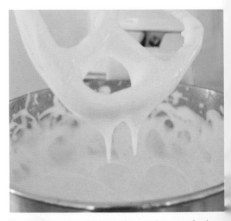

Step 4: When the mixture is the consistency of cake frosting, it is ready to be jarred.

LEMONGRASS, COCONUT AND ALOE HEALING WHIP

This final coconut whip takes a little more prep time, but the result is a lovely, healing lotion for your skin. The fresh lemongrass scent with the cooling aloe and luxurious coconut oil is a fantastic combination. The tough part about this whip is processing the aloe. The aloe plant has a gelatinous gel inside its leaves and there is cooling, healing power in that gelatinous juice. Utilizing fresh aloe gives this lotion a nice, light feel and added health benefits. Plus, you only need three ingredients for this whip!

YIELD—1 TO 2 (4-OZ [118-ML]) JARS

¼ cup (59 ml) aloe juice (extracted from aloe leaf)

1 cup (230 g) solid or ½ cup (118 ml) liquid coconut oil

10 to 15 drops of lemongrass essential oil

Mesh sieve or applesauce processor

Mason jar or small glass container

1. You will need to either find an aloe plant to grow or grab a giant leaf at your grocery store. I found a giant leaf for $1.29, which was double what I needed for this recipe! Aloe plants are also easy to grow and propagate at home, so either way will work!

2. To extract the gel and juice, split the aloe leaf down the middle and scrape out all of the gel and juice from the inside into a small saucepan. Remove the gel from the juice at this point in the recipe, squeezing the gel until you have ¼ cup (59 ml) of aloe juice in the saucepan.

3. Add the coconut oil and heat on a low temperature on the cooktop until the oil has melted. You will have a total of around ¾ cup (177 ml) once melted

4. Transfer the mix to a stand mixer and let it do its job! Mix, mix, mix and then whip, whip, whip as soon as the coconut oil starts to solidify. This is an easy task to accomplish while emptying the dishwasher or waiting for water to boil on the stove. If you just stand there watching the mixer, it might take a year and a day for the coconut oil to start to harden up.

5. Stop the mixer and add in your lemongrass essential oil. Give it one more little mix, then push the mixture through a mesh sieve or applesauce processor, pushing down on all the little bits of gel to make sure you get as much aloe goodness as possible out of the mix. Throw the leftover bits of gel into the compost pile.

6. Package your whipped oil in a sealed Mason jar or small glass container and store in the refrigerator. Use within 6 months.

Find large aloe leaves in your local grocery store if you cannot grow them.

Split aloe leaf to access the gel and juice.

MANGO, COCONUT AND BEESWAX LOTION BARS

Remember the lotion bars we made in the previous chapter? Those rose and citrus bars are delightful, but *this* recipe is my favorite hands down. You can use various butters and oils, and add various essential oils for different scents, but this recipe doesn't need any extras. I do not use any additional scents for these lotion bars because the light scent is just perfect! Also note that this recipe uses white or bleached ingredients. If you use a darker yellow beeswax or shea, the result will be a deeper yellow bar. Both are beautiful!

YIELD—10-12 LOTION BARS

1 cup (400 g) beeswax pellets

1 cup (500 g) mango butter or shea butter (I used mango for this recipe, but shea works as well!)

1 cup (230 g) solid or ½ cup (118 ml) liquid coconut oil

Microwave-safe bowl or small crafting crockpot for melting

Additional scents (optional)

Oiled molds

1. Place the beeswax pellets, mango or shea butter and coconut oil into a microwave-safe bowl or small crafting crockpot.

2. Melt slowly, stirring often. The oil and butter melt much faster than the beeswax. Take your time and continue to melt at a low temperature. The beeswax *will* melt and incorporate! *Do not allow the mix to boil*. This will change the chemical makeup of the soap and the mixture can explode.

3. If you're adding additional scents, do so now! Once the mixture is completely liquid and no solid bits remain, give the mix another gentle stir and slowly pour into molds. The liquid is very hot, so please wear gloves if you are working with hot lotion for the first time. If you spill any little bits, they will solidify quickly. Simply peel them off the countertop or side of the bowl and remelt.

4. Allow the bars to fully harden. You may then use immediately! No waiting period required!

LET'S TAKE A MINUTE AND DISCUSS INGREDIENTS.

First of all, note that the name of these bars indicates strong tropical scents, but this is not the case with the finished product. Rather the scents of the oils, butter and wax used are subtle. The scent of these plain lotion bars is beautiful, but not strong. For an intense mango or coconut scent, you will want to add additional essential oils or chemical scents. I chose to leave the bars as-is and enjoy the subtle scent of this luxurious and completely natural bar.

When making these bars, note that you can substitute various butters, as long as you keep the ratios the same. Shea butter works very nicely. Also note that I suggest beeswax pellets as opposed to slabs. The beeswax melts very slowly compared to the coconut oil and mango butter. A slab would take a long time to melt, while the pellets are slightly faster. Don't try to omit the beeswax completely though because it provides the structure to the bar that makes it solid at room temperature!

CHAPTER 16

SUGAR & SALT

Do you have a sweet tooth? Most of us do, if we are honest with ourselves. It is only natural! The sweetness of sugar might be a curse to our dieting plans, but it is a cheap and easy-to-find addition to your crafting arsenal. Salt is even cheaper and easier! In this chapter, I will show you how to plant your own sugarcane, gather your own sea salt and make a variety of scrubs for every mood you happen to be in.

HOW TO GROW SUGARCANE

When you think of growing your own sugar, you probably picture sugarcane, right? Sugarcane is in fact one of the classic sweet plants, but corn syrup and sugar beets also make up a portion of the sweetening industry. Sugarcane is the base plant for both rum and molasses and if you chew a chunk of it, you will taste sweetness along with those deeper molasses and rum flavors. You will also get a mouthful of woody pulp, which you must spit out. It is terrible for your digestion!

Sugarcane is actually quite an easy plant to grow, but it is difficult to process. It is part of the grasses family, so like bamboo and even lawn grass, it is a monocot, meaning it has one "blade" rather than multiple leaves on a stem. Those "blades," however, are *huge* on sugarcane. The canes will grow in clumps, each blade growing from the cluster of roots underground.

To start a new sugarcane plant, buy a cane as fresh as possible from a local market. If you cannot find it at your normal grocery, try a health food store or Asian marketplace. You are looking for healthy, fat "nodes" on the joints of the cane. This portion of the plant is incredibly tough and full of growing material.

Use a machete or ax to cut on either side of each joint, separating the cane into long, smooth pieces and several chunks of joints. Bury the joints directly into a pot with rich potting soil and water in. Water once a week with 2 to 3 cups (473 to 710 ml) and place in direct sunlight. You should see a sprout emerge from the ground in a few weeks. Note that sugarcane is a tropical plant and will only do well outdoors in zone 10 and up. If you have a greenhouse or atrium, you can try growing sugarcane in a pot over the winter indoors. If you want to just experiment and see what happens, you should definitely try even if the plant will not last very long!

To process full grown sugarcane, you have two options: squeeze or cut. Squeezing the sugarcane is very difficult, but this is the method commercial growers use to make molasses, rum and pure sugar cane juice. From the juice, syrup or crystallized sugar products can be made. While juicing can be done with heavy duty equipment at home, I find it easier to use the fresh sugarcane when cut as fun swizzle sticks or meat skewers!

Sugarcane grows from these nodes, so make sure they are present when planting.

Sugarcane plantations used to crush the cane in presses like this one at the Botanical Gardens in Caguas, Puerto Rico. There are now no functioning sugarcane plantations in Puerto Rico.

SUGARCANE SWIZZLE STICKS AND SKEWERS

After the joints from the sugarcane are removed, the smooth middle segments will be left over. These can be processed by traditional pressing, but I suggest you go the easier route of cutting. Once cut into sticks, the sugarcane makes a great meat skewer (think shrimp!) or swizzle sticks for fruity tropical drinks. Let me show you how!

Smooth, meaty sections of sugarcane (no joints)

Machete or sharp butcher's knife

Cutting surface outdoors such as wood, concrete or strong tile

1. Cut the joints out of the sugarcane with a machete.

2. Hold the chunk of sugarcane vertically and cut outer skin off with a machete or sharp knife. It helps to make a small notch first, wedge the machete or knife into the cane, lift up both knife and cane gently and tap lightly down the side of the cane.

3. Once the skin is removed, you will have a nice chunk of sugarcane ready to cut into long, straight pieces. Carefully cut with kitchen knife or chop with machete.

4. Use a knife to shave away any loose pieces, then rinse under water for a smooth stick.

5. Use the sticks as swizzle sticks for an added burst of rum-like sweetness or use a skewer for shrimp or chunks of fish on the grill. Make sure you soak skewers in water as you would with bamboo skewers so that they do not burn.

Remove joints from the cane.

Remove outer skin with a machete.

Remove any bits of peel left over.

Use a machete to cut chunk (pictured) into swizzle sticks.

HOW TO HARVEST SEA SALT

Salt is perhaps the most basic of food accoutrements and without it, everything is simply bland. While good old table salt will suffice for most of our culinary needs, there is a growing trend of place-specific sea salts harvested by artisans. Each particular region is said to have a definable, specific taste, so connoisseurs of sea salt love tasting the differences between the salts of various oceans, from the Florida Keys to the arctic Pacific to the coast of Maine. My particular sea salt comes from a little beach we call Glass Cove in Humacao, Puerto Rico. If you live by an ocean, perhaps you would like to try your own salt harvest!

Salt water source (clear of industrial waste, pollution runoff and fossil fuels)

Clean towel

Clean gallon jugs

Cooler, baking sheet or other flat container

Large bowl

Wooden spoon

Storage jar

1. It is important to select a section of ocean that is clear of industrial waste, pollution runoff and fossil fuels. You can have the water tested or simply find a secluded, wild spot that you know is clean.

2. Gather as many jugs of sea water as you wish, going as deep into the ocean as you can to minimize debris.

3. Pour the water through a thick towel into a large bowl to get any algae, small pebbles and sand out of the water. Squeeze the remaining saltwater from the towel into the bowl.

4. Place the seawater into a flat container, such as a rimmed baking sheet or cooler in the hottest, windiest place you have. The sun and wind are your evaporation vehicles.

5. Alternatively, you can boil down the water as you do maple syrup, but to use gas or electricity seems a bit wasteful. However, this method is much quicker!

6. Once the water has been boiled off or evaporated, there will be a crust of salt left in your container. With a wooden spoon, scrape it into chunks and allow it to continue drying out.

7. Hit the chunks with your spoon to crush into small bits and store in a glass jar. Enjoy the taste of the sea!

WHAT KIND OF SUGAR OR SALT IS THIS?

WHITE CANE SUGAR

This is your typical, white table sugar with a nice fine grain. It can be used in any of these recipes, though other sugars might work better. If your sugar scrub is too loose, you can always add a little plain white cane sugar from the pantry to give it more structure!

TURBINADO SUGAR

This pretty brown sugar is marketed as more "natural" because it has not been processed down as much as typical white cane sugar. The natural molasses has not been taken out of the sugar, creating the rich brown color. I don't know if I buy the health benefit claims of turbinado sugar, as it is still sugar from the cane, but I love it as an ingredient for beautiful sugar scrubs. Note the moisture content of turbinado sugar is higher than white cane sugar and will affect recipes accordingly.

BROWN SUGAR

Unlike turbinado sugar, brown sugar has molasses added *in* to the sugar once processed to create the color. Brown sugar has a distinctive taste and is more sticky and clumpy than white cane sugar.

COARSE SANDING SUGAR

This sugar has larger grains and is rougher on the skin than white cane sugar. This is a wonderful thing when creating an exfoliating scrub! Coarse sanding sugars also look gorgeous on top of baked goods or as a topper for smoother sugar scrub mixes.

TABLE SALT

This fine-grained white salt has been on American tables for decades. Buy the cheap stuff when crafting!

KOSHER SALT

There are various types of kosher salt, but I prefer the large coarse grains for eating. They can also be fantastic for crafting! "Regular" kosher salt has a finer grain, but also has a shaved texture making it an interesting addition to scrubs. It is not as uniform as regular white table salt. Note that when it comes to salt, "kosher" is mainly referring to the salt as an ingredient for "kosher*ing*" meats and such. It is not identified as truly kosher for those of the Jewish faith unless it says "kosher certified salt." Kosher salt typically does have fewer additives than regular white table salt, but what we are going for is the texture of the salt.

ROCK SALT OR ICE CREAM SALT

This salt has huge, chunky grains. Note that there is rock salt and then there is *rock salt*. The rock salt used to melt snow has tons of impurities and actual rock fragments in it. Do not buy this to use for crafting. However, there are some rock salts and ice cream salts in the baking aisle that are basically just sodium chloride in a large grain. Check the box label to see whether it is classified "edible." This also goes for pickling salt.

THE SALTS

In Chapter 3, we talked about rosemary salt, but almost any herb or spice can be added to various salts to make interesting textural combinations. Try combining your favorite salt to whatever you have growing in the garden and experiment with creating meat brines and rubs. Here are a few of my favorite combinations!

KOSHER SHAVED SALT, CORIANDER AND DRIED CILANTRO

Did you know coriander and cilantro come from the same plant? Coriander is the seed, while cilantro is the fresh leaves. This plant is very easy to grow from seed and perfect for beginners! Harvest the leaves when they are young and the seed once the plant has withered and died. Dry either or both and add to a nice shaved salt. Use liberally!

ICE CREAM SALT AND VARIOUS DRIED PEPPER SEEDS

This thick-grained salt works well as a brine and with the addition of various hot and sweet pepper seeds from your garden, this brine can get *hot*! Try it on pork, beef and even for vegetables like kimchi.

COARSE GRAIN KOSHER SALT AND PEPPER

Salt and pepper! A classic combination upgraded to elevate even your most basic culinary dishes. Try growing black pepper or pink peppercorns in your garden for the freshest taste. Combine in a grinder with coarse kosher salt grains in equal portions and you will never go back to a plain set of shakers again!

When combining salts with herbs and spices, the ratios are very flexible and depend on your taste preferences. Do you prefer your food incredibly spicy? You might add more peppers or cayenne to a salt mix. If you like your food mild, you might try the cilantro and coriander salt mix with a ratio of 1 tablespoon (15 g) herb to each cup (292 g) of salt. Experiment and enjoy!

Culinary grade rock salt can be used for homemade salt scrubs, but stay away from salts meant to melt winter ice.

HOW TO CREATE BASIC FLAVORED SUGARS AND SALTS

Sugar and salt are both vehicles for using many of the plants grown in your garden. Flavored salts and sugars can be used for cooking, but they are also in luxurious scrubs for the hands and feet. The ingredients below can be used both in cooking and in the scrubs featured later in the chapter. You will need to fully examine the baking aisle at the grocery store to experiment with different types of salts and sugars. All are affordable and each adds subtle differences to each sugar mix. Join me as we explore these pantry staples and pair them with home-grown herbs and spices!

VANILLA SUGAR

Vanilla might be the most difficult sugar of the bunch, but it is still not particularly hard to make. Do not be afraid of the price of real vanilla beans as they add incredible flavor for just a tiny bit of product. I would advise you to buy vanilla beans straight from growers online as opposed to purchasing them at the grocery store through traditional re-packers. The price hike is immense! Once you have purchased some vanilla beans and picked up sugar at the grocery store, the process is easy and the result is delicious!

8 to 10 vanilla beans

Knife

2 cups (400 g) sugar

1. Simply cut your vanilla beans into two halves and use your knife to scrape out the inside. Get every little bit! Discard seed pods.

2. Add the beans to a bowl with the sugar. Make sure you add the beans to the sugar and not the other way around as your precious vanilla bean paste will be wasted by sticking to the sides of the bowl.

3. Mix well and store in a canning jar. This will last between 3 to 4 months.

CINNAMON SUGAR

Cinnamon sugar is highly underrated as a culinary ingredient. Add it to almost anything and the dish will taste better. Ask any child whether regular old toast or cinnamon sugar toast is superior. There is no question—cinnamon rules. Cinnamon is a very light powder when ground and combines best with a light, grainy sugar. Good old-fashioned white cane sugar is your best bet for this mix! The larger grained sugars will separate from the cinnamon, making the mix clumpier. Granted, it will still taste yummy, but white sugar and cinnamon combine for a perfectly even flavored sugar.

White cane sugar

Cinnamon

Jar for storage

1. Combine 3 parts white cane sugar with 1 part cinnamon in a pretty jar.

2. Shake, shake, shake until completely combined, though be careful the lid is on tightly or you will have a massive mess on your hands!

3. Tie with a bow and you are finished.

NOTE: Cinnamon can be used in low amounts in sugar scrubs. However, those with sensitive skin should avoid it. Cinnamon oil should not be used on the skin directly or in large amounts in the sugar scrubs below as cinnamon oil can burn the skin. Use with caution!

ALMOND SUGAR

Of all the flavored sugars in the world, almond sugar is my favorite. It is also incredibly simple, but slightly more expensive than the more pedestrian cinnamon sugar. You will need two basic ingredients: almond extract and turbinado sugar. Both are easily found in grocery stores nationwide. Check out the baking aisle to find both ingredients, with the extract being a little brown bottle stored near the vanilla extract and the sugar among its sugary relatives. Turbinado sugar has a fancy name, but it is basically a cane sugar that is less refined than the white stuff in your sugar bowl. The moisture content is high and it has nice, large grains, making it perfect for sugar scrubs!

Almond extract

Turbinado sugar

Jar for storage

1. Simply add 10 drops of almond extract (*drops*, not spoons!) per cup (200 g) of turbinado sugar and store in a sealed jar. Use this sugar as the base of a sugar scrub or as a yummy topping for muffins or oatmeal!

NOTE: This recipe also works well with white cane sugar, but the turbinado sugar is significantly more beautiful.

USE SUGAR AND SALT TO CREATE LUXURIOUS BATH AND BODY PRODUCTS

Sugar scrubs are fun to put together and fun to use for a luxurious shower. They combine the natural scrubbing power of sugar or salt with fragrant and healing herbs, oils and spices. Try inviting your family or friends over for a sugar scrub making party or package up your favorite combination for gifts!

TURBINADO AND BROWN SUGAR BASE SCRUB

Though sometimes turbinado sugar is confused with brown sugar, they are two different animals. Together though, they make a wonderful mix! Brown sugar gets its color from added molasses while turbinado is simply not refined yet and has not been stripped of natural molasses. The reason for using both in this sugar scrub has nothing to do with the molasses, and everything to do with texture. Combining large and small grains makes a smooth, yet exfoliating sugar scrub that feels delicious on the skin! This particular recipe is a base recipe and will work well with a host of different essential oils. I like bergamot or grapefruit essential oil, but you might prefer clary sage or lemongrass. It is completely up to you! The base itself has little scent, but a lot of texture.

YIELD—TWO 8-OZ (237-ML) JARS OR SEVERAL SMALLER JARS

2 cups (400 g) almond sugar (see page 161)

1 cup (200 g) light brown sugar

¼ cup (59 ml) olive oil

10 to 15 drops of your choice of essential oils

Jar

Mixing spoon

1. Simply mix the ingredients in a large bowl and transfer to a sealable jar. The scrub will keep in a bathroom for 1 month or in the fridge for several.

2. To use, scoop about 1 teaspoon of scrub into your palm. Work into skin and then rinse under running water. Your hands will feel smooth and have a soft coating of oil on them. Gently towel dry your hands.

TURBINADO ALMOND SUGAR SCRUB

This is hands down my favorite sugar scrub. It is thick, not loose, and has a wonderful crumbly texture thanks to the turbinado. The coconut oil is left on your hands after scrubbing, making them feel luxuriously soft. The combination of the coconut scent with the almond? It is absolutely my favorite. It does not get better than this in winter when hands are in dire need of some serious help!

YIELD—TWO 8-OZ (237-ML) JARS OR SEVERAL SMALLER JARS

1 cup (236 ml) barely melted coconut oil

2 ⅓ cups (460 g) turbinado sugar

3 tsp (15 ml) almond extract

Jar and mixing spoon

Flat containers for decanting such as pie plates or a cookie sheet

Containers for storing

1. Melt the coconut oil in a microwave-safe container until just barely melted. 1 cup (236 ml) takes 30 seconds to 1 minute. Do *not* melt oil in original container as it can catch fire in your microwave. Ask me how I know.

2. Place the melted oil into your mixer or large bowl and cool for 10 minutes. Add a small amount (up to ⅓ cup [67 g]) of sugar to see if it melts. You *do not* want the sugar to melt for this recipe. If it does, wait until the oil has cooled further and test again. When sugar stays in solid grains, add the 2 cups (400 g) and the almond extract and mix immediately. This mix just needs to be combined and does not need to "whip" like other scrubs and coconut whips.

3. Decant the scrub immediately into your flat containers. Allow the mix to harden overnight and then use a fork to crumple it into a nice "crumb." Place the crumbled scrub into containers for gifting or storing.

4. To use, scoop about 1 teaspoon of scrub into your palm. Work into skin and then rinse under running water. Hands will feel smooth and have a soft coating of oil on them. Gently towel dry your hands.

SUGAR SCRUB TROUBLESHOOTING

The scrub is too "loose" and goopy. What do I do? Add more sugar! Sugar helps thicken up a mix that has too much liquid in it.

My scrub got really hard last night and I can't break it with my fingers. What do I do? Some scrubs are meant to be thick and crumbly, particularly scrubs with coconut oil that melts onto the skin when used. Use a fork to "crumble" your scrub and scrub onto hands under a little water. If your scrub still seems too thick, try adding a little olive oil (just a little!) to your mix to loosen it up a bit.

I made a really nice sugar scrub, but it formed a crust on top. How do I make sure this doesn't happen? When creating natural products, you are also omitting chemicals that make sure traditional bath and body products shelf stable. However, there are a few things you can do to combat a sugar scrub "crust." Make sure your scrub is tightly sealed between uses and give it a shake now and then. If all else fails, just break the crust with your fingers or a spoon and remix the scrub. A crust only affects the appearance of a scrub, and does not change its usefulness.

The oils and sugars separated in my scrub. How do I make it stay together? The sugar scrub that is most likely to separate is the Chai Scrub (page 166) since it is looser and contains more liquids than the others. Make sure that you allow the scrub to spend a good 2 to 3 minutes in a stand mixture to fully incorporate. If the scrub has already separated, you can use it by giving it a little mix with your finger or spoon. If you would like to fix a whole batch, decant the separated scrubs into a large bowl and heat until warm, but not boiling. Once warm, put it into your mixer and give it 2 to 3 minutes at as high a speed as it can go without splattering. Adding 2 teaspoons (5 g) of cornstarch as a binder will help hold it together.

ALMOND JOY COCONUT CRÈME SCRUB

I know I said the Turbinado Almond Sugar Scrub on the previous page is my favorite, but this one gives it a lot of competition. The addition of heavy whipping cream takes it to another level and literally makes this scrub good enough to eat!

YIELD—ONE 8-OZ (237-ML) JAR

1 cup (236 ml) liquid coconut oil

Stand or handheld mixer, or a strong arm with a whisk

1 tsp almond extract

½ cup (100 g) white cane sugar

¼ cup (59 ml) heavy whipping cream

Jar for storage

1. Melt the coconut oil in a microwave-safe container until it is just barely melted, about 30 seconds to 1 minute. Do *not* melt the oil in the original container as it can catch fire in your microwave.

2. Place the melted oil into your mixer or large bowl and add the almond extract, sugar and whipping cream. If you are using a stand mixer, start with speed 1 or low and as the scrub thickens up work up to about a speed of 6 or 7, which is a medium-high. The scrub should look like grainy frosting at this point.

3. Decant the mixture immediately into your containers. This scrub should be used right away or stored in the refrigerator due to the cream and possible spoilage.

NOTE: I have had no problem with spoilage storing the scrub next to my kitchen sink for the cold winter months, but use caution with warmer temperatures.

TIPS FOR SUGAR AND SALT SCRUBBING

DID YOU KNOW? The skin will absorb more oils and moisturizers when softened with heat. Skin will also slough off more dead skin with warmth, so take a warm shower or bath to open up pores before using a sugar scrub for the best results.

DID YOU KNOW? Leaving your sugar scrub open to the elements will make it crusty on top. Make sure you close that jar up when you are finished!

DID YOU KNOW? You should not try to mix the scrub directly in the jar. Sugar scrubs "melt" when they come in contact with the liquids or oils of the recipes and you will often need to add more sugar to get a nice mixture. Mixing in the jar you will present the scrub in is just asking for more mess and more work! Make up several batches in a large bowl and decant into jars once the mixture is perfect.

DID YOU KNOW? Scrubs are not soap. Please do not wash your hands with a scrub and assume they are clean. While salt and some herbs have cleansing properties, it is not the same as cleansing your hands with soap. Scrubs exfoliate and moisturize, but are not made to clean.

SPICED CHAI SUGAR HAND SCRUB

Oh, chai. Dear, dear chai. Every afternoon, you might enjoy a date with the liquid version of chai and give your hands a scrub down every evening with those exotic spices and deep brown sugars. A note of caution: many of the spices in this particular scrub can be irritating to sensitive skin and the concentrated oils can literally burn your skin. Cinnamon and clove in particular can be quite toxic to skin in concentrated amounts. The amounts used in this scrub are small and in powdered form, so you should not have any problems, but if your skin reacts easily to foreign substances, skip this one! I have used this scrub on my hands with no problems, but would hesitate to use it as a full body scrub.

YIELD—THREE 4-OZ (118-ML) GLASS JARS

2 cups (400 g) almond sugar (plus additional sugar if needed) (see page 161)

1 cup (200 g) light brown sugar

½ cup (118 ml) olive oil

½ cup (80 g) cinnamon sugar (see page 161)

2 to 3 tbsp (30 to 60 g) star anise water, boiled and cooled

1 tsp each of chai spices, such as powdered clove, ginger, fennel or classic cardamom (your choice of favorites!)

Jar and mixing spoon

Containers for storage

2 tsp (5 g) cornstarch (optional)

1. Mix the ingredients in a large bowl and transfer to a sealable jar. If the sugar scrub is "loose," add more sugar until the mix will "spoon" like cookie dough. If it looks more like brownie dough than cookie dough, keep adding sugar and mix, mix, mix! A turn in a stand mixer for a few minutes really helps this scrub to incorporate, but a strong arm and whisk will also do the job.

2. Allow the scrub to settle overnight in your mixing bowl and if the oil has risen to the top, it needs to be warmed and mixed again. *Do not boil* mixture, but warm it up 30 seconds at a time in the microwave, stirring each time. Once warm, mix, mix and mix again. Add the cornstarch if your scrub has a hard time staying together and continues to separate. This scrub will keep in a bathroom for 1 month or in the fridge for several.

3. To use, use a spoon or scoop to place around 1 to 2 teaspoons (7 to 15 g) into the palms of your hands. This particular scrub is too loose to just use your fingers to scoop. Scrub well under running water until all remnants of spices are rinsed away. Gently towel dry.

NOTE: To create star anise water, boil 15–20 star anise pieces in ¼ cup (60 ml) of water, allowing the mixture to boil down to a concentrated 2–3 tablespoons (45 ml).

CANDY CANE SUGAR SCRUB

We are now ditching the brown sugars for pretty white sugars and scrubs that show off ingredients well due to the high color contrast. The white sugar is also very fine and makes for a softer scrub than the thicker brown scrubs. This scrub is a perfect Christmas stocking stuffer as the candy canes give a festive red and white speckled look. Just make sure gift recipients don't mistake them for candy!

YIELD—15 TO 20 SMALL STICKS

1 cup (236 ml) liquid coconut oil

Microwave-safe bowl

2 cups (400 g) white cane sugar

2 crushed candy canes

Jar and mixing spoon

1. Melt the coconut oil 30 seconds at a time in a microwave in a microwave-safe bowl.
2. Allow the oil to cool slightly and then add the oil to the sugar, stirring vigorously.
3. Allow the mix to cool completely and crumble it with a fork.
4. Add the crushed candy canes to crumbled sugar scrub.
5. This scrub molds particularly well, so you can simply add it to a jar or you can create fun shapes. I like to use silicone ice cube trays to make peppermint scrub "sticks" or simply roll them into little "snowballs" that you crush and scrub with in the shower.
6. To use the scrub sticks, simply break off a piece, scrub between your hands, rinse and dry.

LUXURIOUS LAVENDER SALT SCRUB

I much prefer a sweet sugar scrub to a harsher salt scrub, but they definitely have their place in the bath and body aisle. Here is my favorite variation that tempers the roughness of salt with smooth coconut oil. The gelatin helps give structure to the salt scrub, but you can make a looser scrub without it.

YIELD—1 CUP (120 G)

1 cup (200 g) mixed salts (I used coarse grain kosher and ice cream salt)

½ cup (118 ml) liquid coconut oil

¼ cup (50 g) unflavored gelatin (optional)

10 drops of lavender essential oil

2 tbsp (15 to 30 g) of fresh or dried whole lavender flowers (as much or little as you choose)

Microwave-safe bowl

Jar and spoon for mixing

Containers for storing

1. Mix all the ingredients, except for the fresh lavender, in a small microwave-safe bowl and then warm it up 30 seconds at a time until the coconut oil melts down. Alternatively, you can heat up the coconut oil separately and add to the mix once it is liquid.
2. Stir all the ingredients well and allow the mixture to harden overnight in the mixing container.
3. Crumble the mix with a fork, stir in the fresh or dried lavender and decant it into small containers. To use, place scrub on hands with a small amount of water and scrub! The salt will exfoliate, the lavender will scent your hands and the coconut oil will remain on your skin, leaving it luxuriously soft!

section six

GROW A HAND-CRAFTED CHRISTMAS CELEBRATION

We will end this book with gifts because, while crafting is fun, the real joy comes when you are able to gift something beautiful or useful made by your own hands. There is no better time to stock up the natural craft supply closet and start creating than around Christmas, when gifts are customary and the cold weather shoves us all inside together. Peeled leaves off the old magnolia, gathered pods, stalks and seeds and a little stolen green from the pines will keep the craft pantry chock full.

Join me as we turn old plant parts into pretty jewelry, imprint beautiful leaves into clay gifts and celebrate those stalwart evergreens that provide structure for the winter garden. Whether you plan to keep your creations or gift them all away, I hope you find ideas that make you want to grow, gather and craft.

FROM SEA TO SHINING SEA, THERE IS A MAGNOLIA YOU CAN GROW

Magnolias. Dear, old Magnolias. Is there anything more classically Southern than a grand old Magnolia? I was thrilled when we moved into our home and there was an old, established magnolia on the property. Then the winter hit, and I remembered we were not in Alabama. No, we are in a solid zone 6, a Pennsylvania garden with Pennsylvania winters and I worried for my magnolia. My magnolia seems happy, but if you would like to play it safe, there are plenty of magnolias to choose from that like their winters a little chilly. Magnolias are beautiful in the garden while blooming, but also offer up winter structure and interest. Their benefits don't stop there though. Gather up both leaves and seed pods from this majestic tree to make everything from earrings and fairy garden accessories to creative gift adornments and table settings!

THE MANY VARIETIES OF MAGNOLIAS

SAUCER MAGNOLIA

Sometimes known as "tulip tree," the saucer magnolia is actually quite different from the *actual* tulip tree with tulip shaped leaves. Rather, this harbinger of spring goes full on *Clueless* pink each year and puts on a show right about the same time the redbuds start budding and popping. A small forest of all the pink flowering cherries, magnolias and redbuds would be a magnificent sight, wouldn't it? Grow Saucer Magnolia in zones 4 to 9.

STAR MAGNOLIA

A common magnolia up north, the Star Magnolia is a small tree grown in zones 4 to 8 and produces darling little fuzzy buds and pretty white flowers in early spring. It was one of the first trees to bloom in two of my previous gardens and I always forced a few branches late in winter. This charming tree can really anchor a small garden design and is an excellent choice for a city garden.

KOBUS MAGNOLIA

The Kobus, hardy in zones 4 to 8, is a beautiful magnolia, covered from top to tip with almost entirely white blooms each spring. Native to Japan, this deciduous magnolia can grow all the way up to 70 to 75 feet. It is not for the faint of heart.

LOEBNER MAGNOLIA

Put a Star Magnolia and a Kobus Magnolia together and you get a Loebner. Grown in zones 5 to 8, this multi-trunked tree is fantastic for the landscape and has pretty pinkish white flowers.

SWEETBAY MAGNOLIA

This is the *one* type of magnolia that can take a little bit of wetness at its feet. If you have a slightly soggy location, but are dying for a magnolia, this might be the plant for you!

YULAN MAGNOLIA

Native to China, this magnolia tops out at around 40 feet (12 m). Creamy white or ivory blooms on the Yulans made them the perfect starting point for breeding the yellow blooming magnolias we have today.

BUTTERFLIES MAGNOLIA

A favorite of gardeners, this magnolia has beautiful yellow flowers each spring on leafless branches. It literally looks like little yellow butterflies dancing on the branches. This magnolia is not particularly great for craft supplies, but it looks *fantastic* in the garden. This magnolia is currently sitting at the very top of my must-have plant list and if you visit Stonecrest next year, you might just see a few!

ANISE MAGNOLIA

Native to Japan and grown in zones 4b to 9a, this magnolia is a good choice for gardeners in colder climates. This magnolia is quite similar to the Star Magnolia and provides cute fuzzy flower buds for crafting and forcing into bloom indoors in the late winter.

SOUTHERN MAGNOLIAS

Remember where we started this chapter? Big, beautiful trees with huge, fragrant white flowers that *scream* Southern USA. They are the queen bee of the magnolia family and offer up those gorgeous blooms in late spring: beautiful waxy leaves all year round and pretty little pods closed in spring and popped open in fall. If you can grow one, it would be a shame not to. They grow well in zones 7 to 9, but you can push it to 6 if you have a warm microclimate.

This is simply a sample of the many magnolias, which includes 80 species native to the United States and Southeast Asia. They are a fun group of plants and offer a lot of bang for your buck in the crafting and ornamental garden. If you can grow one, you absolutely should. Let's talk about how to do that.

GROWING AND CARING FOR MAGNOLIA TREES AND BUSHES

Established magnolias are pretty tough and do not require much babying. The biggest thing you need to remember is to make certain any pruning is done at the correct time. Though magnolia leaves and pods are great for crafting, the *flowers* are the real show stealer. If you prune the trees too late in the year or into early spring, you will prune the flower show right off. If you need to shape a magnolia, do so immediately after it flowers in spring so that it will have time to put on new growth and flower buds for next year. Dead wood can be pruned at any time. Magnolias do not need heavy pruning as a rule, so simply prune for shape and use the clippings to make the crafts below!

YOUNG MAGNOLIAS

If you are starting a magnolia from seed or simply planting a young tree, you have a bit more to think about. Though magnolias are tough, they *do* have preferences and a happy magnolia means a happy gardening crafter (or crafting gardener, whichever way you lean).

If you are starting a tree from seed, look for a seed pod with the brilliant orange seeds already starting to release. This means they are fully ripe. Plant immediately into rich potting soil and water until moist but not soaking. Water again when the top of the soil dries out. Once your seed sprouts, slow down watering to once every few days and offer indirect sunlight. Repot to a larger container if roots start to appear out of the bottom drainage hole. Once the seedling is 1 to 2 feet (30–60 cm) tall, plant in an area that has nice, rich soil that drains adequately. Magnolias do not like wet feet! Make sure that you do not crowd the magnolia with other plants, particularly under the canopy. Magnolia roots are fairly shallow and they will have a hard time thriving if you are constantly digging around and puncturing those shallow roots. Most magnolias like a little bit of sun and a little bit of shade. They are happy on forest edges and in partial shade in ornamental gardens.

You might also have to stake your new seedling if it does not stand tall on its own. If necessary, stake it before the roots form and do not move your magnolia once settled. The success rate of transplanting mature magnolias is very small.

PROPAGATING MAGNOLIA

To propagate magnolia, you might consider air layering. Cut a 1 to 2 inch (2.5 to 5 cm) slit in a healthy, growing stem and pull a bit to expose the inner plant. Wrap the wound with sheet moss and secure with plastic wrap as a "bandage." After several months, check to see if new roots have developed. If so, the new plant is ready to be detached from the mother plant and planted in the ground.

Alternatively, you can ground layer a low-growing healthy stem by wounding it slightly (not cutting it completely through) and laying the wound under 2 to 3 inches (5 to 7.5 cm) of soil and secured with a rock. The plant will grow roots in the soil and after 2 to 3 months it should be ready to transplant. The easiest process to propagate a magnolia is to simply plant the bright orange seeds that pop out of fertilized pods in fall, but the success rate is rather low. Plant many seeds for a few plants and transplant when the plants are 4 to 5 inches (10 to 12 cm) tall, have a solid root system and several sets of mature leaves.

CRAFTING WITH MAGNOLIAS

While some magnolias, such as the Star Magnolia or Butterflies, lose their leaves each winter, others are fully evergreen. The classic Southern Magnolia is the latter. Those big, beautiful waxy leaves are the perfect flexible, yet tough and hardy crafting material. The pods, or fruit, of all magnolias also offer plenty of room for crafting experimentation. Join me as I show you some of my easy favorites!

DID YOU KNOW? Magnolias are pollinated by beetles, not bees! There is no nectar in the flower, but plenty of pollen that beetles carry around from bloom to bloom.

MAGNOLIA POD "TREES"

Have you ever taken a magnolia pod and held it upside down? They look like little trees! Add these trees to fairy gardens (see pages 12 to 21), use as toppers for a woodland cake or add to a child's diorama. Unopened seed pods work best for this craft.

Magnolia pods

Green paint

Paintbrush

Cardboard with small holes for drying

1. Gather unopened pods and if necessary, rinse with water. Allow them to completely dry.

2. Hold the pod by the stem and paint.

3. Stick the stems into a cardboard box as a drying rack.

4. Repeat with 2 to 3 more coats of green for full coverage.

Magnolia pods that have opened already are best for making little painted "trees."

DID YOU KNOW? The White House used frosting-covered magnolia pod "trees" for the 2010 Gingerbread House!

5-MINUTE OR LESS MAGNOLIA LEAF CRAFTS

MAGNOLIA LEAF FEATHERS

The leaves of magnolia take well to paint and the shape is quite feather-like. The end result? A fun rainy-day activity for kids and adults alike! You can add these fun feathers to a child's headdress, create a little wreath or use as place cards at your next family gathering!

Simply gather fresh green magnolia leaves that are damage free. A few brown spots are okay! Wash and dry leaves completely and cut little feather notches into the sides at an angle. Exercise your creativity with switches and swipes of metallic paint for fun giant "feathers" that will last for months!

PLACE MARKERS

Classic Southern Magnolia leaves provide a nice large writing surface and have a waxy coating that a permanent marker skims right over. This makes them the absolute perfect leaf for creating name tags on a Thanksgiving table or for using in outdoor games. Think scavenger hunts, clues left by fairies and even a variation of capture the flag with multiple marked leaves hidden throughout the garden. The ideas are endless!

MAGNOLIA WREATHS

Magnolia wreaths are a classic garden craft, and the possibilities with arrangements are wide and diverse. Try combining both green and golden brown magnolia leaves for a natural look, go gold for a glittery winter wreath or experiment with placing stems down into a foam wreath for a deep 3D wreath. Have you ever seen a magnolia cross? Magnolia leaves are rigid, yet flat, so they will hold their shape, yet lay nicely into a shaped form. Attach them to a cross frame for a lovely Easter decoration!

MAGNOLIA BUNTING

Consider creating a fall or winter bunting out of brown magnolia leaves or use fresh green leaves for a spring mantel décor. Simply string the stems by knotting each leaf onto a long length of twine and decorate leaves with metallic marker or paint.

MAGNOLIA SEED EARRING DROPS

These little earrings are very inexpensive, cute and quick to create. Made from the fuzzy seed pod pieces of an unripe pod, the earrings are unique, textural and make a great little gift. Make sure you seal them though, because without a sealer, they are quite fragile!

Jewelry pliers (if used lightly, regular pliers will do in a pinch)

"Closed" fuzzy magnolia seed pod

2 head pins or ring/eye pins

2 small- to medium-sized jump rings

2 fishhook earring wires (lever backs will also work)

Matte spray (not glossy) sealer (I like the one by Mod Podge)

1. Very gently place the tip of your pliers into the "tip" of each seed pod section. Gently push down and then up, without squeezing the pliers. The piece of seed pod will gently "pop" and release, but will crush if you squeeze the pliers together. Remove 8 to 10 pieces per earring. One seed pod will supply plenty.

2. Hold a piece of seed pod in one hand, supporting the back and gently but firmly push a pin (head or eye) through the dark brown portion of the pod piece. Continue with all pieces until the length of the pin is full.

3. Using jewelry pliers, twist a loop to close off the bottom of your eye pin, or create a loop at the top of a head pin.

4. Attach the pin to a jump ring, then attach to your fishhook or lever back earring wire.

5. Seal the earring with the spray sealer to harden and protect. Allow to dry completely

6. Repeat the process for the second earring.

Craft pretty little earrings from the fuzzy magnolia seed pod.

MAGNOLIA VASES

Magnolia leaves are large and beautiful—perfect for hiding ugly vases and showcasing pretty glass vessels. Using this tutorial, turn your everyday vases into beauties on their own or create show-stopping containers for a seasonal floral arrangement.

Fresh, large, green magnolia leaves

Vase

Hemp, string or ribbon

1. Collect fresh magnolia leaves directly from the tree for this project. Once they have fallen from the branches, they will be too brittle to bend easily.

2. Place the leaves into the vase with a few inches on the bottom of the vessel and the remainder of the leaves around the inner circumference of the vase interior. Weigh the middle down with a large stone or glass floral frog.

3. Fill with water and your cut flowers for a beautiful look worthy of wedding place settings.

4. For a longer lasting solution, place leaves inside a large vase, then sink a slightly smaller vase inside. Fill the small vase with water and the dry magnolia leaves will last for weeks!

5. Alternatively, you can wrap the leaves on the exterior of the vase and secure with decorative ribbon or string. Twine makes a natural complement to secure the leaves, while beautiful silk or grosgrain ribbon can make for a slightly more dressed up look.

CREATIVE CHRISTMAS WRAPPINGS AND TRAPPINGS

You know those super expensive cone-shaped trees with leaves layered down the sides sold everywhere and beyond? You know those super cheap Styrofoam cones at the dollar store? You know that magnolia tree shedding leaves at lightning speed outside your backdoor? Do you see where I am going with this?

MAGNOLIA CONE TREES—Those Styrofoam cones cost a buck and your magnolia leaves are free and whether you go shimmering gold or natural green, you can make these expensive décor items for a tiny fraction of the retail price. The trick? Hot glue and *pins*. Use only hot glue and the leaves will be shedding off the cones as fast as they shed off the tree. Use only pins and the leaves will be curling up or down around the edges as they dry instead of lying flat. You need both! Simply pin them by the top point onto the Styrofoam form, then hot glue under the edges to secure. You may spray with a sealant to make the project last a bit longer, but this step is not necessary.

MAGNOLIA CHRISTMAS CLUSTERS—Have you lost the love for a real live Christmas tree and the needles it leaves all over your carpet every year? Not quite ready to have a fully artificial tree? I have the compromise for you. Get the largest fake tree your home can hold, and if you are buying fake, get it pre-lit for Pete's sake (literally if your husband's name is Pete). *Then*, go gather up a bunch of magnolia branches with all the leaves and pods still attached. Get big long branches, not short weaselly branches. Now, stick those bunches of *real* foliage in the holes of all that *fake* foliage and *voila*! You have a woodland tree ready to deck! Added bonus: Cleaning up the random, large magnolia leaf or two that falls off the tree is *worlds* easier than getting every last pine needle off the floor.

MAGNOLIA GIFT WRAPPINGS—Want some beautiful gifts that will look right at home under your woodland tree? Consider both the leaves, pods, seeds *and* branches of the magnolia. The brilliant orange-red seeds can be glued in beautiful little Scandinavian designs against a nice white or gold wrapping paper, while the leaves look just perfect in a starburst on natural colored paper. Take your craft punches to town on your magnolia leaves (they can take it). Little leaves, little Santas or a modern grid of squares goes incredibly textural when punched from living plant materials. Why not try a red butcher's paper with brown leaf cutouts? A simple little branch with two little leaves and a jingle bell tassel? Perfection.

MAGNOLIA WINTER GARLAND—Magnolias make a fantastic garland with other winter trimmings, such as pine or spruce. They also make a stunning piece all on their own if you have enough to spare. (*Remember not to prune a young magnolia too much!*) Again, if you are working with a nice fake garland, the addition of natural magnolia leaves and other organic materials can push it right over the edge from tacky to *awesome*.

MAGNOLIA WREATH—Have you seen a magnolia wreath? Ever? Search for it on Pinterest. There are thousands of ideas. My favorites are the minis. Take a single new branch of magnolia with tiny leaves and twist it around to a 3 to 4 inch (7.5 to 10 cm) circumference. Secure with floral wire and put them *everywhere*. Complement these little wreaths with wreaths of rosemary and bay and your home will look and smell as if you have landed in Geilie's attic. (*Outlander.* Read it.)

Magnolia leaves are tough enough to be punched! Any paper punch can make cute leaf confetti, and larger punches can create shaped name tags or place cards.

CHAPTER 18

PINES, FIR, SPRUCE & OTHER NEEDLED EVERGREENS

Evergreens play a significant role in the design of your garden and in the framing of your home on its property. Whether it is three miniature cypress trees in a window box or a forest cradling a stone manor, evergreens are an integral addition that maintains form and color through spring, summer, fall and of course, winter. You might not immediately think of these common bushes and trees when it comes to crafting, but they provide natural materials in abundance and they offer their bounty all year long.

HOW TO CARE FOR NEEDLED EVERGREENS

In the spring, summer and fall, evergreens are the background players in the garden. They offer a solid green backdrop for blooming peonies, roses and mums. However, their value in winter is even greater, as they offer the only bit of green outdoors amidst fields of dead brown and frosty white. You can ignore evergreens for most of the year, but in winter they need a little more help!

You might not think of giant, stalwart evergreens as being infantile, but when it comes to winter winds, heavy snowflakes and chilling ice storms, they can be. In fact, aside from your roses and any plants that are not rated cold-hardy for your zone, your evergreens are going to need the most care this winter. Why? Well, the reason is simple, really. They hold onto their leaves, their needles, which causes much more weight from freezing rains, and much more desiccation than other plants. Desiccation is the moisture loss that evergreens suffer, particularly when the winter winds are brutal.

COMBAT WINTER DESICCATION

Evergreens need water in the winter and newly planted evergreens need copious amounts of it. Make sure you water in new plants well and provide additional water whenever the ground is not frozen and precipitation is inadequate. Browning needles are a sign your evergreens need water immediately!

Mulch is your best friend for any plant that you are hoping to help with water needs. After adding several gallons of water to your evergreen in fall, cover with 1 to 2 inches (2.5 to 5 cm) of mulch, making sure to not touch the actual bark of the tree. The mulch will help conserve water from evaporation when winter winds are fierce.

Don't give up on brown needles! Often, evergreens will show signs of desiccation, but the plant can survive. If the entire tree has turned brown, you are out of luck, but if you only have slight browning of some needles, simply prune for appearances sake, water well and allow new green growth to fill in during the spring.

SAVE THE TREES FROM OLD MAN WINTER

Freezing rains will be the worst enemy of your evergreens in winter. The ice will coat branches and any weak or over-burdened branch will snap, causing plenty of damage to the tree and possible damage to surrounding structures. What can you do? Well, there is not much you can do about the ice, but you *can* help when snow starts to pile on *top* of that ice. Your evergreens and weak-crotched trees like Bradford Pear, get very heavy with ice and snow. Simply knocking large drifts of snow off with a broom can save a tree.

When you lose the battle to ice, if you can help it, wait until spring to do damage control. Pruning in winter is always hard on trees, so unless the branches are not resting on your car or your roof, the pruning can wait.

SPRING REVIVAL FOR THE EVERGREENS

In spring, evergreens need water, water, water and a light pruning. Most plants can handle a pruning of up to a third of growth, but evergreens are a bit more finicky. Stick to pruning only up to a quarter of the entire growth of the tree or bush. If the spring rains are plentiful, there is no need for additional water. If your spring has been light on precipitation, give those thirsty evergreens an extra drink!

CRAFTING WITH EVERGREENS

Mature evergreens provide massive amounts of raw material for you to use in crafting. Whether you are using the pinecones to create pretty candle melts, the needles to press designs into clay or just that fresh scent of Christmas pine, there are plenty of reasons to harvest crafting materials from your forest this year!

NOTE: If you live in a climate where the temperatures range from warm to hot and back again, say zone 8 or 9, your biggest concern will be water during droughts for your evergreens. Aside from water needs, your evergreens will need little intervention!

DIY PINE CANDLE MELTS

Do you love the smell of candles, but hesitate to put burning flames indoors? I have a very simple solution for you! *Melts*. Melts are simply flats of wax, full of essential oils that release their luscious scents when warmed. Creating DIY melts is a simpler project than creating your own candles and they are far safer. An additional benefit is the ability to add "solids" to your melts that would otherwise burn in a candle. Think evergreen branches, spruce needles and even paper flowers! You will need a few simple supplies and a candle warmer to use the melts when complete.

Paraffin or soy candle wax, or previously-used candle ends (unscented or Christmas scents)

Small crafting crockpot or double boiler

Candle warmer

Pine scent (or any essential oils or scents you choose!)

Small bits of spices, herbs or plants such as pine needles, star anise or cinnamon sticks (optional)

Various glass jars and containers (new or second-hand)

1. Melt 2- to 3-inch (5- to 7.5-cm) chunks of wax in a small crafting crockpot or double boiler. Alternatively, melt old candles in glass containers on a candle warmer. The total amount of wax should be about ½ to 1 cup (118 to 236 ml) at a time. Stir until completely melted and fully liquid. Do not boil!

2. Add in 10 to 30 drops of essential oil per ¼ cup (59 ml) of liquid wax, along with any spice, herb or plant "bits." Little pieces of pine needles, beautiful whole star anise or whole cinnamon sticks are beautiful and don't run the risk of catching fire like they do in a candle. If you would like the "bits" just on the top of the candle, wait until the top is still soft, but starting to firm up and drop little bits into the warm wax. Remove any prickly bits that stick out once the melt is completely hardened.

3. Stir the mixture gently and pour into clean, thick glass jars. To create layered candles, simply pour one color or scent at a time and allow it to harden slightly before adding the next layer. Pour the wax slowly to keep the layers a straight line across the jar. Pouring hot wax into thin or cold glass containers can make them shatter, so use strong, room temperature glass. Vintage glassware from the thrift store is often a good bet! Also, hot candle wax can burn, so please pour gently and carefully. You can always use a plastic funnel if you are worried about spilling.

4. Allow the wax to harden and cool in the jars until firm to the touch. If you let the wax harden completely, the wax can actually be taken out of the containers as small individual melts.

5. To use the melts, simply set them on a candle warmer in their jars or containers. As the wax melts, the house starts to smell amazing!

VARIATION: PAPER FLOWER MELTS

Want to add beautiful toppers to your melts? Try paper flowers! Thick paper will stand up to being literally encased in wax or simply attached with a little hot wax on the bottom. Wait until your wax starts to solidify and is "jiggly" like Jell-O, then place a paper flower on top and gently press down. To encase the petals in wax, very gently add additional hot wax over the top of the flower!

BLEACHED PINECONES AND OTHER NATURAL FINDINGS

Pinecones and cinnamon sticks are classic Christmas decorations, but sometimes traditional needs a twist. Those classic natural elements just need to take a bleach bath for a fun new look! Join me as we "go blonde" with these easy-to-find natural crafting goodies. For information on gathering pinecones and acorns from nature, see page 42.

Pinecones, cinnamon sticks, magnolia seed pods, acorn tops, etc.

Glass jar

Heavy item to weigh down items

Pure bleach

1. Place your various natural bits into a glass jar.

2. Weigh down the items with a piece of wood or other heavy item that will not be damaged by bleach.

3. Pour straight bleach over the cones until they are fully covered.

4. Allow the mixture to sit 24 to 48 hours until it turns a deep brown.

5. Discard the browned bleach or use it to kill garden weeds. Remove cinnamon sticks (if using) to dry and place new bleach over the pinecones for a second bath. Magnolia seed pods also need just one bath while acorns take 2 or 3 like the cones.

6. Allow another 24 to 48 hours for the bleach to fully permeate the cones.

7. Use the bleach to kill weeds again, or simply discard, then lay the cones out to dry and reopen. The cones will still look a bit brown and will be tightly closed. As they dry, the color lightens up and the cones open again.

8. Once dry, the bleached cones, pods and sticks will not stain nor smell. They look fabulous on various gifts, hung in trees or on wreaths.

*See photo on page 180.

Day 1: Bleaching pinecones.

Day 2: Empty dark liquid and add more bleach.

Day 3: Repeat if necessary.

A CELEBRATION OF THE GARDEN— HANDMADE GIFTS

After collecting, growing, harvesting and crafting with the plants in this book, you might decide to gift some of your creations! Take the dried lavender flowers, rosemary stems or citrus slices, the freshly gathered acorn tops or leaves from your tropical plants or evergreens to press and preserve. One of my favorite ways to preserve plants from the garden is to highlight their shapes via clay or concrete. These projects just happen to make nice little gifts as well! Join me as I give you an introduction to clay and concrete stamping and let your creativity run wild with gift ideas! From jewelry and home accessories to bath and body products or kitchen accoutrements, gifts that include and highlight plants are always a welcome present.

HOW TO IMPRINT LEAVES ONTO CLAY AND CONCRETE

When you decide to start experimenting with clay and cement, you must get the right supplies. In fact, nothing will determine your success or failure more quickly than the decision you make at the checkout counter. Clay *must* be oven-dry clay, specifically for jewelry projects if you want your pieces to last. Cement *must* be a quick set or your plant presses will not last long enough to leave a sharp imprint. You can use recycled materials for molds, you can pick plants from the side of the road and you can use thrifted wire, cord or straps, but the actual clay or cement *must* be an exact purchase. No cheating! Let's start with clay, shall we?

IMPRINTING CLAY JEWELRY PIECES

Imprinting leaves onto clay takes an element of nature that dies within a day or two and gives it life for many years. The beautifully designed petals, leaves and stems can be captured and enjoyed in jewelry pieces or small home accessories. The brand of clay I use is Sculpey, and the best price I have found is online at Consumer Crafts. You can also find oven-bake clay at crafting stores and might stumble upon a clearance. When you pull the clay out of the package it is *very* hard and difficult to work with. This strength makes it a great product later on, but dictates the necessity of an adult crafter. Serious hand strength is required to "work" this clay, but there are a few things that will help.

1. Heat, but not too much. A little bit of heat loosens up the clay enough to make it workable, but do *not* place it in an oven or microwave. You *do not* want to bake it before the project is complete. Rolling the clay in your hands provides a bit of heat, but typically, I cut small one-inch chunks and let them sit in the sun for 30 minutes or so before rolling.

2. Go small! Those one-inch chunks are important! You will want to cut the clay into small pieces before attempting to work it as a large piece will take forever to work down.

3. Avoid contaminants like dust, plants, pebbles, etc. When you are getting started with the clay, you must not allow any contaminants to get into it because they make the clay doubly difficult to get working. *Do not* roll the clay on a concrete surface, dusty tabletop, etc. Roll in your hands!

4. A clay press might just be your best friend for clay projects! For small beads and baubles, rolling beads in your hands will work perfectly well. However, making uniform, flat pieces out of clay is quite difficult and a press makes quick work of it!

5. Once you have gotten the clay loose and warm, you can start forming it into shapes. Use a clay press to make flat sheets to cut with cookie cutters, roll some balls or elongated beads in your hands, or use a mold. Let's start with a couple simple projects that utilize *natural* molds.

Various seed pods can make interesting molds for clay. Experiment with your forest finds!

CLAY AND LEATHER BRACELET

This is a perfect project to start with if you are crafting with kids or don't have any experience working with clay. It is a great introduction to both clay and pressing, and the result is quite lovely. This piece is done in two basic steps: bead making and assembling. Once the clay is dry, it is hard as a rock and the addition of a soft leather makes a nice contrast. Let's get started!

1 square inch (2.5 sq. cm) of high quality oven bake clay

Detailed leaf with graphic veins

Toothpick

18 inches (46 cm) of leather string or strap

1. Roll the clay chunk in between your hands until perfectly round and smooth.

2. Pick a small, detailed leaf with graphic veins.

3. Lay the leaf in your hand, place the ball on top and gently press the edges of the leaf up and onto the bead.

4. Roll the bead in your hands gently, but firmly, to imprint the leaf and maintain a round shape.

5. Remove the leaf immediately by pulling directly up from the stem.

6. Insert a toothpick toward the top third of the bead and twist as you puncture the clay.

7. Bake the bead at 275°F (135°C) for 30 minutes.

8. Remove the toothpick and thread the bead onto a strap of leather.

9. Wear as a necklace or loop around wrist for a pretty, dangly bracelet.

NOTE: Multiple beads can be made simultaneously and you can create interesting bracelets, necklaces or even small rings using the same techniques!

ACORN CHARMS

I was using an acorn cap to cut a perfect circle out of clay, then turned it around and loved the way the clay looked nestled perfectly into the cap. Acorn charms were born! Acorn charms can be attached to wire, string or strapping for jewelry, places on a key chain, nestled in fairy gardens or simply placed in a bowl for your desk.

High quality oven-bake clay, such as Sculpey (I used brown)

Large, empty acorn caps

Various leaves for pressing

1. Roll the clay between your hands into a perfect ball. Roll quickly to work up heat and fold the clay back into itself if cracks develop. Continue folding and rolling until there are no cracks.

2. Place the ball into an acorn cap. Turn over and press gently onto a flat, clean and smooth surface. Continue pressing gently and turn the acorn cap to trim the edges of extra clay. Turn the acorn cap over for pressing.

3. Gently press a leaf into the clay, making sure all portions of the leaf have made contact. Thin leaves will turn translucent when pressed. Make certain the entire stamping area of the leaf turns translucent before removing.

4. Gently lift leaf straight up and off the clay. Do not pull sideways as the pressing might smear.

5. Bake acorn charms in a 275°F (135°C) oven for 30 minutes to set.

CLAYNUTS TUTORIAL

Do you remember when those rocks with inspirational words first came out? Peace. Love. Harmony. Relax. They were everywhere for a few years, but seem to have tapered off. While playing around with various natural molds, I came up with a fun replacement—a claynut! Two claynuts placed back-to-back can hold a "secret message" inside, a single nut can hang on a leather loop around your neck or held in your hand as a talisman. These little nuts also make great family name "stones" for fairy gardens or just a little reminder to "relax" on your windowsill.

High quality oven-bake clay, such as Sculpey (I used brown)

Large, concave empty nut pod, such as walnuts or hickory, macadamia and Brazil nuts

Metal letter stamping kit

Clay tool or small knife

1. Roll a smooth ball of clay and place into the nut pod.

2. Flip pod over and press gently onto a flat, smooth and clean surface. You should have a flat and smooth "writing surface" now.

3. Use metal stamping letters to press the word, name or numbers of your choice into the flat portion of the clay.

4. Trim off any extra edges with a clay tool or small knife.

5. Pop the "nut" out of the shell/pod and bake at 275°F (135°C) for 30 minutes. Alternatively, you can bake the clay *in* the nut pod and leave it as.

*See photo on page 186.

CEMENT, CONCRETE AND HYPERTUFA

Once you have mastered clay, you might want to try the slightly more difficult process of making cement, concrete or hypertufa. Since they are often confused, let's start with a few definitions.

CEMENT

Made from limestone, iron and aluminum, among other ingredients, this stone-like mixture is heated, then ground into a flour-like substance. Combined with water, cement forms a solid, stone-like surface.

CONCRETE

Always made *with* cement, concrete is a blend of rocks, sand and other aggregate held together with cement.

HYPERTUFA

A lighter-weight product that sets and looks similar to concrete, but has light, natural products mixed into the cement instead of all heavy stone and sand.

The project that follows is made from my own blend of hypertufa. My recipe includes:

- » 2 cups (473 ml) quick set cement
- » ½ cup filler (236 ml) such as perlite, vermiculite or soil
- » ¼ cup (236 ml) water

Simply mix your ingredients in an old bowl, then quickly place the solution into a mold that is either non-stick and disposable or oiled. Note that most DIY molds will be ruined after one setting, so don't use your nice dishes! Cardboard boxes, plastic recyclables and old tins make wonderful molds, so you do not need to run out and buy expensive ones. If the mold cannot be easily pulled or ripped away—like cardboard—you might want to give it a spray of cooking oil to make it release quicker.

NOTE: The recipe above is for a small batch and can be doubled or tripled. I typically mix up small batches one by one instead of large wheelbarrows full.

GEOMETRIC HYPERTUFA PLANTERS

Our three boys received Teenage Mutant Ninja Turtles as presents and they came in the most fantastic plastic packaging. The size was just right for a small planter and the shape was a fun geometric design. You can use any plastic recyclables you might have to make your own unique planters!

Plastic mold

Cooking oil spray

Leaves or plants for imprinting (optional)

2 batches of hypertufa (see page 191), divided

Small pot

1. Oil your plastic mold with cooking spray. Add in any leaves you want to impress upon the bottom or sides of planter. The larger and more detailed the plant is, the better it will press in hypertufa. Imprints will *not* be as crisp as they are in clay. Small, delicate leaf presses will not show up at all. I had the best luck with large fern-like leaves.

2. Mix up a small batch of hypertufa and pour gently into mold until it is halfway full. Lift and drop the planter gently onto your work surface a few times to release any bubbles in the hypertufa.

3. Immediately oil and place a small pot into the center of the planter and mix up a second small batch of hypertufa. Pour around the edges to complete the planter.

4. Dry overnight or longer until the mix dries from a dark gray to a very light, whitish gray.

5. Plant succulents or any low-water plants in these small, geometric planters and give to your favorite friends! (Jade is a great choice!)

Pour hypertufo into oiled form, halfway up the sides.

Place a small pot in the mixture and fill around the edges with hypertufa.

Remove pot once the planter is dry.

LACE AND NATURE CROWNS

These little crowns are quite simple to make and are the perfect vehicle for pretty bits from nature! Older children can wear the crowns for imaginative play, while infants look just darling posed in a crown for a few photos. You might just love this project so much, you make one for yourself!

Thick lace, 1-2 inches (2.5–5 cm) wide

Scissors

Fabric stiffener

Vase or other round, glass item to mold crowns

Various natural bits, such as rosebuds, dried flowers, fresh flowers or seeds

Needle and thread or hot glue

1. Measure the lace so that it fits around the forehead to the back of head with 2 inches (5 cm) of overlap. Cut to size.

2. Soak the lace in fabric stiffener until it is fully saturated.

3. Place the lace around a glass vase bottom or any other round object so that the lace forms a circle. Overlap the ends to connect.

4. Allow the crown to dry for 24 to 48 hours until it is fully dry and stiff. The ends should be secured together, but if they fall apart, simply hot glue them together or re-soak and form the crown again on the form.

5. Use a needle and thread to attach various natural bits to your crown, weave dry or fresh flowers into the lace or use hot glue to permanently affix small dried buds or seed pods.

6. Wear and enjoy!

Mold lace on a similar sized round glass vase to fit child's head.

Prep flowers by stripping leaves from the stems.

Cluster florals and secure with twine before attaching them to the lace crown.

RESOURCES

While many of the main components of these crafts are found in the garden or woods, almost all crafts require additional tools and supplies. The first place I start is thrift stores and garage sales. Craft supplies are often at both (folks clearing the clutter!) and they lose value very quickly in resale. In fact, like books, craft supplies are almost always 75 to 90 percent off retail prices when sold secondhand. A few second-hand favorite finds of mine include my wood burning tool for 25 cents, thick black denim fabrics and outdoors fabrics for just a few dollars up in Amish country and too many candles and glassware to count! When creating the Pine Candle Melts, consider a trip to the thrift store first for candles that are way beyond their prime. They are always marked very cheaply when they have been burned and that leftover wax is exactly what you need!

When I cannot find what I need secondhand, my two go-to sources are Amazon and ConsumerCrafts.com. Full disclosure, I design crafts for Consumer Crafts, so I am always aware of new and clearanced products there, but they also often have the best price available online on many products. I use Amazon Prime and make sure that any craft materials I buy are included with Prime for free shipping. The costs are right at or slightly cheaper than brick and mortar stores. With my four small children, heading to an actual craft store is not a peaceful, nor practical event, so I do most of my shopping online. If you are able to run out to the store, Michael's has everything you could ever desire for crafting and run great clearances. Jo-Ann Fabrics has fantastic deals on fabric remnants as well as seasonal décor you can pull apart for crafting. Pat Catan's and A.C. Moore are also great craft supply stores, but are regional and may not be in your state. Also, don't discount Wal-Mart, Target or Kmart! Kmart runs massive sales on seasonal products, Target always has a few craft or party supplies on discount endcaps and Wal-Mart remnant fabrics can be quite nice and very cheap! On the following page I've listed a few specific sources for hard-to-find supplies.

SOAP BASES

Oatmeal, glycerin, goat's milk and shea are available for $9.99 at Consumercrafts.com.

SMALL CRAFTING CROCKPOT AND CANDLE WARMER

I often see these for pennies at garage sales. Electric fondue pots work too!

ESSENTIAL OILS

Amazon. Food-grade essential oils are the best and I often buy them in large kits to get the best deal. Note that some essential oils are quite expensive, while basic oils like peppermint are cheaper.

SHEA BUTTER, MANGO BUTTER AND BEESWAX

Amazon! Search for the best price on Amazon and make sure you use Prime for free shipping. I have never found these items cheaper than they are on Amazon. However, you might have a local beekeeper with inexpensive beeswax, so you might want to ask around before buying online.

COCONUT OIL

Costco sells a giant tub of coconut oil and it is by far the best price. The oil is the same quality as smaller batches from different brands, so I now stick to Costco. You can also find coconut oil easily on Amazon if you do not use club memberships.

TOOLS

ConsumerCrafts.com offers hands down the best prices on crafting tools. If you cannot find the tools at a yard sale, Consumer Crafts is the place to go. All of my jewelry supplies, cutting machines, heat tools, hot glue, etc. come from Consumer Crafts.

MOLDS FOR CANDLES AND SOAP-MAKING

I rarely buy these new. Many thrifted jars, glasses and silicone pans make perfect soap molds and candle containers. Be open minded and shop for pennies instead of dollars!

For detailed shopping lists and links, visit www.craftingwithnature.com/resources.

ACKNOWLEDGMENTS

Thank you...

To Mom, Dad, Nana, Pop, Aunt Jill and Miss Monica for caring for the children so that I could steal away to write. To Stuart, Thomas, Henry and Penelope, for sharing their craft room with their mom and sharing her time with this book. To Ball Seed and Burpee seed for opening their test gardens for photos and for their freely given expertise. To the Southern Living Plant Collection for thriving plant samples to photograph. To Bonnie Plants and the Garden Bloggers Conference for sponsorship and collaboration. To Sheila Schmitz at Houzz, for teaching me to write concisely. For Sarah Kubelka at Crafts Unleashed, for helping hone my tutorial style. To Kate Walker for assuring my recipes worked and for first sharing the book secret. To Lauren Lanker, for modeling the courage to write a book. To Beth Bryan for encouragement, contacts and a mutual love of plants. To my freshman English teacher, who once told me I wrote like Boo Radley; motivation comes in many forms. To Sarah Monroe, for putting up with and encouraging this first-time author. To Will and the Page Street team for taking a chance on this first-time author. To Jan Berry, for riding this tide together.

To Alex, for everything.

ABOUT THE AUTHOR

AMY RENEA is a freelance writer, photographer, gardener and crafter. She is the owner of the crafting and gardening blog A Nest for All Seasons, which won the *Better Homes and Gardens* Reader's Choice Best Gardening Blog award in 2014. Amy has written for Houzz, Hobby Farm Home, *Celebrating Everyday Life* magazine and FORBES.com. She also owns the submission sites Looksi Square and Looksi Bite. Amy splits her time between central Pennsylvania and the Southeast coast of Puerto Rico. She lives with her four children, husband Alex and a small flock of backyard chickens.

You can find Amy on her website (anestforallseasons.com) or on social media:

Twitter @amyreneak

Pinterest.com/amyk

Facebook.com/aNESTforallseasons

INDEX